ALL TIME HEROES

FROM ALL TIMES

~ Volume 7 ~

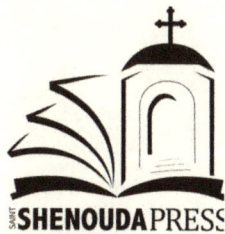

SAINT **SHENOUDA** PRESS

All Time Heroes

from All Times

~ Volume 7 ~

The Life of Saint Victor
Son of Romanus

ST SHENOUDA'S MONASTERY
SYDNEY, AUSTRALIA

2017

All Time Heros from all Times - Volume 7

THE LIFE OF SAINT VICTOR SON OF ROMANUS

ST SHENOUDA MONASTERY
8419, Putty Rd,
Putty, NSW, 2330
Australia

www.stshenoudapress.com

ISBN 13: 978-0-99445710-6-9

Cover Design:
Hani Ghaly,
Begoury Graphics
begourygraphics@gmail.com

Contents

The Life of Saint Victor

*Here begins the martyrdom of saint Biktor
(Victor), the general and martyr, the man glorious in
Christ, the wearer of the crown in very truth, who
completed his glorious strife on the twenty-seventh day
of the month Pharmoute. In the peace of God. May his
holy blessing come upon us, and may we all be saved
together. Amen.*

The Emperor and his decree for idol worshipping

It came to pass in the third year of reign of Emperor Diocletian that the Devil led his heart astray from God, and made him do things that were not appropriate. Diocletian worshipped idols. He thrust the God of heaven behind his back, for the sake of creatures made of wood and stones and for the sake of vain things that were fashioned by the hands of men. Listen now to the account of the young man called Victor.

Emperor Diocletian took counsel and decided to do things that were unseemly before God, Jesus Christ. He made seventy images of gold, and named them after 'gods.' To thirty-five of these he gave names of gods, and to thirty-five, the names of goddesses. The number of his other gods and goddesses amounted to one hundred and forty.

Emperor Diocletian affixed a decree on the outside of the door of the Palace, wherein was written: 'I, Emperor Diocletian, hereby command that from Romania in the north to Pelak (Philac) in the south, every man, whether he be Governor, or general, or count, or bishop, or elder, or deacon, or reader, or servant, or free man, or soldier, or countryman, shall worship my gods. Any one who shall say, "I am a Christian," shall die by the sword. As for all you noblemen of high senatorial rank, who hold office in connection with the Palace, you shall enforce this decree in such a way that every man shall worship my gods. These are the gods who give us victory in battle, and it is they who are the protectors of ourselves. These gods give you and the whole army strength and, therefore, he that does not rise up early in the morning, and come at dawn so that we may go into the temple together and offer up sacrifices to the gods, he shall be cast into the sea, so that all men may know that I am king, and that there is no other king besides me.'

It came to pass at dawn, on the first day of the month Pharmoute, that Emperor Diocletian, and his army, Governors and generals went into the temple. The Emperor took his seat upon the throne, and he caused the announcer to make a proclamation, saying, 'O you Roman people, come and offer up sacrifice.' The Emperor made an altar of silver and a vessel of gold in which to burn incense; and he made a great pedestal of gold, on which to place the statue of Apollo. The Emperor commanded to bring frankincense, the finest flour of wheat, the purest oil, and a rare old wine, to pour them out upon the altar on which was blazing fire. Afterwards they lighted two hundred candles on golden candlesticks, four hundred candles on silver candlesticks, and two hundred white horses drew his gods into the temple.

When they brought his gods into the temple, Emperor Diocletian stood up on his throne, lifted his crown off his head, set it upon the head of the statue of Apollo, and bowed down to worship it three times, saying, 'You art the god who lives, O Apollo, the greatest of the gods, who gives us victory in war.' After the Emperor worshipped Apollo, his three fellow Emperors, Romanus, Basileides and Euaios, came and worshipped Apollo also. Now they held equal rank and power with the Emperor and the Emperor loved them exceedingly. He had given to each one of them fifty centenarii (coins) of gold, in addition to the most noble rank of generals in the army. Now Diocletian said to them, 'O my fellow Emperors, I hope you would be persuaded by me, to worship my gods. You yourselves can see this great festival which has spread abroad everywhere this day. I swear by the salvation of my strength, and by the salvation of the seventy gods, and by the strength of the great god Apollo, that I will make the whole world worship my gods. The festival, which is being celebrated this day, shall be proclaimed throughout the whole world. You yourselves shall give propitiatory offerings and gifts to the temple of Apollo, besides those which the Governor and the generals shall give.'

Romanus gave thirty centenarii of gold, Basileides gave twenty, Euaios gave ten and the Emperor gave sixty. In total, they gave one hundred and twenty centenarii of gold as offerings to the temple of Apollo. The Emperor also gave three precious jewels, set on the crown of Apollo, and they were of exceedingly great price.

The Emperor said to Romanus, the General of the Army, 'Offer up sacrifice to my gods.' Romanus went forward and offered up sacrifice together with his two fellow Emperors, as did the other nobles who were attached to the Palace. On that day, six hundred thousand soldiers and two million people of the country worshipped Apollo.

It came to pass that Basileides, Head of the State, would not worship the gods of the Emperor. Thus, Diocletian put him to death together with his entire household. The whole city was greatly shaken by the thronging of the multitude, men died, being choked by the fumes of frankincense, and by the smell of incense, which the people were offering on the altar. Those who died through being crushed by the multitudes were five thousand in number, in addition to those who died in the temple, who were also five thousand in number.

Emperor Diocletian went about the whole city, saying, 'When you have finished offering up your sacrifices, you shall eat and drink at the door of the temple of Apollo and Artemis, and you shall glorify them, for it is they who have made the heavens, the earth, the sea and all mankind.' The Emperor went back to the Palace at the time of the morning meal, and he called Romanus the general and said to him, 'Take this edict, and make the rest of the multitude offer up sacrifice.' Romanus, the general, took the edict from the hand of the Emperor, and he gave orders to the people, saying, 'O Romans, offer up sacrifce.'

VICTOR AND HIS REJECTION OF IDOLS

When all the people had offered up sacrifice, it was the turn of Emperor Romanus' son, Aba Victor, to offer up sacrifice. Now his son was a young man nineteen years of age. He worshipped God and held His commandments in fear. He was a virgin in body; he ate once each week and prayed all night long. He hated the world. He did not drink wine; neither did he eat food cooked with fire. He did not decorate his person, and he did not adorn himself with rich apparel and fine clothing. He did not mount the horse that was used in a chariot. He never gave utterance to an obscene (or, insulting) word, and never, under any circumstances, did he swear an oath by anything or by anybody. Whenever he heard of a

Christian in distress, he would minister to him, and give him whatever he had need of. If he saw any one naked, he would strip himself of the garment which he had on him, and give it to him. He performed all the commandments and fulfilled all the instructions in the Gospel of our Lord Jesus Christ.

Now his father wearied him exceedingly, saying, 'I shall take the daughter of Basileides as a wife for you,' for his father and Basileides had made an agreement in respect of her. The agreement involved two hundred centenarii of gold, four hundred centenarii of silver, ten menservants, ten hundred maidservants wearing golden bracelets, four hundred horses, ten hundred mules, ten hundred camels, ten hundred farms which were under labour and ten hundred ships which sailed the sea.

The blessed Aba Victor would not be persuaded by his father or Basileides, and he said to them, 'All these things shall perish.' Aba Victor kept himself for the kingdom that is in the heavens. The Lord Jesus was accustomed to appear to him, face to face, and He loved him because of his purity. The noble Victor made for himself a small chamber in his house and there he would retire to be free from the company of his parents. He had not slept upon a couch since he was fifteen years of age. He prayed by day and by night, and he fasted from one sabbath to another. He attended the assemblies for Holy Communion. He prayed one thousand and sixty-five prayers during the day and seven hundred and thirty prayers during the night. His food consisted of bread and salt only.

The Devil tempted him with carnal desire, for he wished to make him fall into fornication; but noble Aba Victor vanquished him by means of prayers and fasting. His fellow noblemen were always making a mock of him, saying, 'Why do you not eat? Why do you not drink? Why do you not wear fine apparel and put on beautiful clothing? You will die, and then others will consume your possessions.' But Aba Victor was accustomed to answer them, saying, 'Clothes become moth-eaten, gold and silver crumble away and the beauty of the body becomes destroyed in the tomb.'

Aba Victor was accustomed to go into his chamber and to pray to God in the following manner: 'O Lord, hear me! O Lord Jesus Christ, You know the speech of heresy, and You know whether I love You or not. O my Lord Jesus Christ, do not permit the love of women to rise up in my heart, lest Satan find a place of abode in my heart, and lest my enemies rejoice over me, and lest You Yourself become angry with me.

Let Your loving-kindness bear patiently with me, and do not remove Yourself from me. Glory be to You, O Father, Who is in the Son, and to You, O Son, Who are in the Father, and to You, O Holy Spirit, for ever, and ever, and ever! Amen.'

Romanus, the General, then said to Aba Victor, his son, 'My son Victor, it is your turn to worship the gods of the Emperor, especially Apollo, the greatest of the gods.' Aba Victor looked into the face of his father, saying, 'O my father, has foolishness obtained a hold of you this day so as to make you forsake the God of heaven? Remember, therefore, that which our Lord Jesus said in the Gospel, "Whoever denies Me before men, him will I Myself deny before My Father, Who is in the heavens, and before His holy angels." Do not therefore deny Him, O father that He may not deny you (Matt 10:33) . God gave a commandment to Moses, saying, "Speak to the children of Israel, "Do not be like the nations who worship creatures instead of Him. Do not lift up your eyes to the heavens, to worship the sun, and moon, and stars. Do not worship the feathered fowl of the heavens, and the four-footed creatures of the earth, for in that day I will destroy you, says the Lord." Now therefore, O my father, do not be like them, lest God destroy you. By the truth of God, O father, I grieve on your account. It would be better for you that you had never been born than that, having been born, you should live and make yourself a man without God.'

Whilst Aba Victor was saying these words, all the soldiers of the army were looking on him and on his father. Then Romanus said, 'O my son Victor, listen to me, and offer up sacrifice. I have never given you an occasion to grieve from your childhood up. Remember, O my son Victor, that I am seeking after your bride, and I am going to take her for you as a wife in the very next month which is coming.' Aba Victor said to his father, 'I have not asked you for a bride or for a gift, but I am grieving exceedingly for you, for you have denied the Saviour. In very truth, you are a miserable man, for the works which you are doing, God hates. Now woe and confusion shall come upon you, because David said, "He who is in a battle, and he who carries away spoil, the same share appertains to both alike." (1 Sam 30:24) Moreover, O my father, the man who commits sin, and the man who is of the same opinion as the man who commits it, the same disgrace appertains to both alike. I beg you therefore, by every means, do not do this thing. Get away from this sin that leads to death. Look into the Gospel of the Lord, and see that while the Jews were crying out "Crucify Jesus", Pilate the Governor took water, washed his hands,   and made himself free from liability for His death.' (Matt 27:24)

His father was filled with indignation, and he swore an oath, saying, 'By Apollo, the greatest of the gods, I will deliver you over to the Emperor so that he may destroy you. Do you not know that I am well acquainted with the matter in which you are occupied? You have learned to work magic in this Name of Jesus. Think not, O Victor, that He will be able to help you, for many men of your kind have died for His sake, and they have been stripped of their worldly goods and estates and possessions.'

Aba Victor answered and said, 'My father, the fruit of the Devil has taken deep root in you.' Romanus then said to Aba Victor, 'Do you not know, O miserable one, that when a man is disobedient to his father, they put him to death?' Aba Victor said to his father, 'Yesterday you worshipped God and I was your son; but today I am not your son, because you have made yourself disobedient to God, and you worship idols. Paul the scribe did say, "Admonish a heretic once or twice and if he does not listen to you, let him alone for his portion is not with the Lord." For this reason, you are not my father.'

Romanus said to him, 'Hear me, O my son Victor.

Do not throw away and waste your early manhood. Do not disgrace yourself in the midst of the imperial palace, and before the whole of the Emperor's army. I myself shall be put to shame because of you, and shall be disgraced before the Emperor. They will take away your rations, and the Emperor will be angered because of you.

However, if you listen to me, I will make an appeal to the Emperor on your behalf, and he will make you a General, and you shall be a man of dignity and honour. Do not be disobedient to me, O my son. Do you not know that your mother and I have no other son except you? O my son Victor, I swear by my own health, that on the day on which you were born, I made an offering of twenty centenarii of gold to the temple of Apollo. On the third day after you were born, I betrothed the daughter of Basileides to you for marriage. Therefore I swear by your own health, O my son Victor, that if you will worship the glorious gods of the Emperor, I will give you a gift of thirty centenarii of gold, in addition to the other things which I am determined to give you.'

Basileides and Euaios went to Aba Victor, and they said to him, 'Truly we came to entreat you this day as a free man. Will you then make yourself become as it were a slave before us? Why has your heart turned its gaze aside in this manner? Why have you not obeyed your father who has asked a request from you? Do not put our hearts to shame, who bow humbly before you.' Aba Victor became angry, and he cried out, saying, 'I swear by the prayers of the saints, for I am not worthy to take an oath by the name of God, that if you would give me the whole world, the kingdom of Diocletian, his possessions and his gods of gold and silver, which he has made, I would not offer up sacrifice. For it is written, "If you should gain the whole world, and lose your soul, what does it profit you?" (Mark 8:36) Do you not know that for the last twelve years I have fasted the whole week through, from Sabbath to Sabbath, and that I have never once washed in a bath?' When Romanus heard these things from his son Victor, he said, 'I swear by Apollo that I will deliver you into the hands of the Emperor, and he shall destroy you. It is written, "When a son is disobedient to his father, they shall slay him."' (Deut 21:18-21) Aba Victor said to his father, 'Behold, that which is written is fulfilled this day, "A father shall deliver his son over to death" (Matt 10:21) If you shall deliver me over to death, O my father, there exists One Who will help me.'

VICTOR SENT TO EMPEROR DIOCLETIAN

The Devil filled the heart of the father of Aba Victor, and he made him deliver Aba Victor over into the hands of Diocletian the Emperor. When the Emperor looked into the face of Aba Victor, he said to him, 'O Victor, why have you not obeyed your father, and worshipped my gods? Is it possible that you do not know that I have absolute power over you?' Aba Victor tore off his golden chain, and removed the badge of his rank and he threw them in the face of Diocletian, saying, 'Indeed I will not wear the badge of an emperor who is mortal, for I wear the badge of the Emperor who is in the heavens. For it is written in the book of the Christians, "It is not possible for you to perform the service of two masters; you must either serve God or mammon," (Matt 6:24; Luke 16:13) And again, "It is not possible for you to eat at the table of the Lord, and at the table of the demons." (1Cor 10:21) Now, therefore, I will serve the God of heaven, and I will not serve mammon, that is to say, you, O Emperor.'

The Emperor said to Aba Victor, 'How do you dare insult me in this fashion? Do you think that there are no instruments of punishment and torture in the prison-house with which I can have you punished? Have I not already commanded you, saying, "Never let me hear this name of Jesus again from your mouth?" An Emperor like myself gave orders to a governor, who put to death your God Jesus, in whom you put your confidence? This king was Herod, who gave orders to Pilate, and Pilate put Him to death. Now, if it was a mere governor who slew Jesus your God, how much more is it possible for me, an Emperor, to destroy this name of Jesus and everyone who worships Him? Now, therefore, O Victor, come, listen to your father, and offer up sacrifice to the gods. If, however, you will not do so, I will banish you, and they shall put you to death.'

Romanus turned towards his son Aba Victor and said to him, 'Are you still not persuaded to pay worship to the gods of the Emperor?' Aba Victor said to his father, 'If Diocletian is your god, good and well; but he is no god of mine, for my Lord is Jesus Christ.' His father was exceedingly angry, and he commanded them to bind his son's arms, carry him outside the city and to spear him there until he died. The soldiers tied the arms of the noble Aba Victor and they fastened a gag in his mouth so that they might carry him outside the city to destroy him.

The Devil took the form of a soldier and he made

himself visible to Victor, and he said to him, 'O Victor, where will you fulfill this evil course of action? By these acts of yours you are abandoning your father to grief. You think that your father hates you. This is certainly not so, for your father loves you exceedingly. Now, therefore, listen to me, and let me tell your father that you have repented, and he will cease to be angry with you. Do not be disobedient to him. Consider Isaac, the son of Abraham, who showed no disobedience to his father when he saw the knife of slaughter. (Gen 22:10) Now, therefore, do not make your father grieve, otherwise you will fall under the curse of Ham, who was under the curse of his father, because he looked upon his father's nakedness. (Gen 9:22) Now, therefore, do not show disobedience to your father, and then I will petition the Emperor, and he will make you a General.' Aba Victor said to the Devil, 'I have not set my mind upon the rank of a General in this world, but upon the kingdom of my Lord Jesus Christ.'

The soldiers told the Emperor that Romanus had passed sentence of death upon his son, Aba Victor, and that his head was to be cut off, because he had sinned against the Emperor and his gods. Diocletian sent two of his bodyguards so that they might seize Aba Victor and bring him to him. The Emperor said to his father, 'I know this day that you do not care neither for your wife nor your son as much as you care for me and my gods, and that you have gone so far as to deliver your only son to death. Hear me and hear the things that I will declare to you, O Romanus. I will throw your son in prison and leave him there until he dies.'

Aba Victor was exceedingly angry, and he said to the Emperor, 'You stupid and senseless Emperor. God shall be angry with you, and He shall send His wrath upon you, and shall destroy your kingdom.' The Emperor was angry, and commanded immediately that Aba Victor be deprived of his rank in court. He made soldiers fasten Aba Victor's hands and they tied him to the tail of a horse. They shaved the crown of his head, suspended a bell from his neck and four soldiers filled their hands with palm branches and beat him. They dragged him naked through the whole city and a herald went before him crying out, 'These things are done to this man because he will not offer up sacrifice to the gods of the Emperor.' On the new moon of Pharmoute, the first day of the month of the beginning of the year, according to the calculation of the Romans,' Diocletian took a sheet of parchment, and wrote on it these words: 'I, Diocletian, who am the Lord of all the World, write to Armenius, the Count of Rakote, that as soon as this man Victor, who is banished, is brought to you, you shall examine him carefully three times, and shall afterwards drive him to the baths and burn him.'

Immediately they delivered Aba Victor into the hands of four soldiers that they may bring him to Rakote. There was an iron collar round his neck, a gag in his mouth and fettering iron about his feet. He was naked as the soldiers drove him along with blows. Aba Victor said to the soldiers who were in charge of him, 'My brethren, I pray you to cease to treat me with such harshness and cruelty, and to upset me so seriously. What is the evil thing that I have done to you, that you should rejoice over me with such keen pleasure? I have never done any injury to you, and I have never committed an act of injustice against you. Do not rejoice over me because evils have risen against me, for it is written, "Do not rejoice over any man who is about to die; remember that we must all die." I served as a soldier with you at one time, therefore do not treat me with insults, and for God's sake remove this gag from me, so that I may be able to say what I want to say to my mother.' The soldiers showed compassion and removed the gag from his mouth as Victor went into his house.

VICTOR MEETS HIS MOTHER

When his mother had seen him, she was greatly disturbed within herself, and she rose up on her throne, and said, 'Is it you, O my son Victor, light of my eyes?' When she saw that he was naked, and that he was wearing iron fetters on his hands and on his feet, she said to him, 'Why are you in this state, O my son Victor? Truly my soul is greatly disturbed when I see you in this state. Are you mad? Could not the Emperor have declared that you pay money, rather than treat you in this way?'

Aba Victor said to his mother, 'Weep, my mother, for they are going to remove the name of Victor from thy house this day. Now, therefore, hear me, my mother. Before everything, fear God, and glorify His saints. Keep holy His sabbaths. Observe the times of fastings. Do not neglect neither the widows nor the orphans. Visit those who are sick. Clothe him that is naked. Give drink to him that is thirsty. Receive a stranger into your house, because from this day onward I myself shall be a stranger. Thus shall the blessing of Sarah be upon you. The things that I have spoken to you, O my mother, may God make sufficient for your soul.

'Now, therefore, O my mother, I know of a certainty that I shall never see you again after this present sight, even if I live. If you hear that I have died, seek after my body and bring it to this place. Do not be like my father who hates his son, but be compassionate. Ascribe glory to God by day and by night, so that He may show compassion to you in the days of necessity. Now, therefore, may God bless you because of the rest which you have given me during the little time which I have been with you; and may my soul rest with you forever! Now I am going to a strange country, and into a city that is not mine, in which I shall beg one person after another, and in which I shall be a helpless and a most miserable stranger. Truly, O my mother, I have become an orphan, fatherless and motherless. If at this present time a man goes away on a journey into a far country, whether in connection with trade or whether for some other purpose, when he comes back after a long time to his house he will find his servants, and his parents, alive; and if he has suffered tribulation in the strange land he will forget his sufferings, because he will find all his people safe and sound. On the other hand, wretched and miserable is that man who, when he goes on a journey into a strange country, must abide in exile until he dies, and indeed, such is my own case this day. I am going to make myself a stranger to you, and to all the people of my house. Swear by your salvation, O my mother, that you will not neglect to enquire after my body. If I die, do not be forgetful of my youth. Remember, O my mother, that I passed nine months in your womb before you brought me forth, and that I drank at your breasts for three years.'

Immediately his mother and his slaves wept for him for he was a kind-hearted man. His mother said, 'Look at me, O my son Victor. What has happened to you? Could not the Emperor have sentenced you to pay a fine of gold or silver, rather than have made you endure these things and banishment to a remote city? Explain to me why it is that you are in this disgraceful state. Explain to me so that I may sacrifice my own life to save you.'

Aba Victor said to his mother, 'All these things have happened to me because of my father, but God shall, in truth, forgive him, O my mother. Had it not been for the Emperor my father would have cut off my head. A stranger has had compassion upon me, and my father has not had compassion upon me this day. Woe to every one who shall obey my father, for their habitation shall be the pit of the abyss for ever, and their father is the Devil.'

His mother said to Aba Victor, 'Do you not know that in the coming month I am going to take a bride for you?' Aba Victor said to his mother, 'O my mother, what use is it for you to bring me a bride, and to put riches of every kind into my hands? It is written, "The world shall pass away and the desirable things of it, but he who shall do the will of God shall abide for ever." (1 John 2:17) Now therefore, O my mother, do the will of God, so that you may live forever. Gold and silver rust, fine attire becomes moth-eaten and falls into holes, a man dies and he turns into corruption in the tomb, and the remembrance of him perishes on the earth. (Matt 6:19) However, the righteous man shall never be moved. O my mother, do not say in your heart that possessions are of value, for they have no value with God. It is God Who can make the poor man a rich man, and the rich man a poor man before the sun shall set this day.'

After these things, Aba Victor departed. He took off the ring which was on his finger, and gave it to his mother, as he prayed to God saying, 'Jesus, my Lord, Who sits upon the chariot of the Cherubim and Seraphim (Ps 18:10; 80:1; 99:1), Whom the angels stand before, Whom the inhabitants of the heavens call "Sabaoth" (Isa 6:3; Rev 4:8), Whom the peoples on the earth call "Jesus Christ," Whom the nations call "Father, Son, and Holy Spirit", keep me steadfast, without fear. Lead me not into temptation, for I am not capable of bearing up against it, but deliver me from the Evil One. To You belong Power and Glory forever. Amen. O my Lord, be with me in every place in which they shall take me for I do not know where they will carry me.'

After these words he blessed his entire household and kissed them. He sealed the door of his bedroom in the Name of Christ Jesus, and came out, and said, 'O my house and my servants, truly I am departing from you. Never again after this moment shall I return to see you. Remember, O my servants, that I have never neglected any one of you, or any stranger. I am not like other young men who are uninstructed, and I have never spoken a word out of place, but I have paid to the humble man the respect that was due to his humble estate, and to the noble the honour that was due to his exalted degree. I have never for a single day manifested any sign of haughtiness and pride, for I knew that each and every one of us must die.'

VICTOR SENT TO THE COURT OF RAKOTE (ALEXANDRIA)

After these things the soldiers put the gag back in Aba Victor's mouth, they seized him, dragged him and put him in a boat. When they arrived at Rakote, they transferred him to prison, and delivered the letter of the Emperor to Armenius, Count of Rakote.

The Duke was in the preaetorium passing sentences of judgment upon the soldiers for the sake of the Name of Christ, and he commanded that Aba Victor should be guarded in prison until the following day. On the next day, when the Count was seated on the judgment throne, in the midst of the marketplace of Rakote, he gave orders, saying, 'Bring to me this profane man Victor, who has been banished here." When they brought Victor before the Count, Victor said to him, "I have been banished to this place for the sake of my Christ. They said, "Offer sacrifice to Apollo"; but I will not offer up sacrifice to fake gods so I have been brought here.' The Duke said to him, 'O bad head! Will you make a mockery of me? By the health of Apollo, this is your punishment: we are to destroy your body by fire. Do you not know that it is the Emperor who has commanded me what I am to do to you? He has commanded me to cast you into the furnace of the baths, but I will show mercy to you for the sake of your father.'

Aba Victor spoke to the Duke, saying, 'I will be bold and will speak in your presence. In times past, before I was delivered over to you, I received rations and money from the Emperor, and I was the fourth officer in his Palace with the rank of Count. After the Emperor, my father was the second in rank in the Palace. If I go on to speak of these things you will say that I am a man of arrogant pride. O Duke, remember the day in which you were appointed Count and entered upon your duties. You made supplication to my father, saying, "Make me Count of Rakote." And my father did not consider you of sufficient honour for the position, and would not discuss the matter with you. Then you entreated me secretly, and said, "Speak to your father on my behalf. Let him take from me three centenarii of gold, and give me the office of Count." I took you into my house, and I made all my slaves wait upon you, and they received gifts of gold armlets from you. After these things my father came in, and I threw myself on my knees before him on the ground, and I remained there until he was persuaded by me, and he made you a Count. Yet you did not keep in mind any one of these things for which you can now repay me. It is written in the Gospel, "He who did eat of my bread with me has lifted up his heel against me.'" (John 13:18; Ps 41:9) The Duke made his men inflict gashes in the face of Aba Victor, and he made them stretch him out with thongs of leather, and they gave him fourteen stripes with the triple flogging whips, saying, 'I will torture you until you die, according to the orders of the Emperor.' Afterwards the Duke made soldiers drive iron nails into Victor's hands and feet, and he covered his whole body with iron, from his head to his feet, and he cast him into prison, where they abandoned him to hunger and thirst until the following day.

When the morning had come, the Count made them bring Aba Victor to him, and every part of Victor's body was loaded with iron fetters. The blessed man Aba Victor was not able to walk because of the weight of the iron which had been placed on his body; and the soldiers supplied twelve men to carry him. When he entered the praetorium, the Duke said to him, 'Can Jesus in Whom you believe deliver you out of my hands? No. Put your belief in Apollo, who is able to save you, and especially in Artemis, the greatest of the gods.' Aba Victor said to him, 'I will not offer up sacrifice.' The Duke commanded his men to raise him up on the wooden framework of the rack. The Duke said to Aba Victor, 'Will you offer up sacrifice or not?' Aba Victor said, 'I will not offer up sacrifice.' The Duke commanded his men to work the rack and stretch him, but Aba Victor did not feel anything at all until the executioners grew exhausted and ceased working the rack. The Duke said to them, 'Why do you not continue to work the rack?' The soldiers said to him, Victor is like a wall and a stone. He feels nothing no matter how much it may be racked."

Victor receives heavenly consolation

The heart of Aba Victor was carried up into the heights of heaven. The angels instructed him concerning the kingdom of heaven and concerning the city of the righteous. The saints saluted him. Abel and Zacharias came up to him, and said 'Greatly distinguished are you, O Aba Victor.' Michael said to him, 'Bear patiently, O valiant athlete. Do not fear this tyrant, for I will be with you and I will deliver you. I say to you that as the angels are accustomed to utter the names of all the saints coupled with their own names, even so shall you be named with the three holy children, Ananias, Azarias, and Misael. Your throne shall be established in heaven before the Lord Jesus. The angels shall rejoice over you, and Jesus shall rejoice upon His throne, and all the saints shall be glad with you.' After these things Michael released the soul of Aba Victor, and it entered again into his body, which was suspended upon the frame of the rack. Michael informed him concerning everything that should happen to him.

VICTOR CONTINUES TO BE TORTURED

Aba Victor resisted the Duke strenuously. The Duke said to him, 'Will you offer up sacrifice or not?' Aba Victor answered him not a word. When the Duke saw that he would not speak, he commanded his men to bring six lighted torches, and to fasten them to his ribs. When they had done this, the Duke made the soldiers bring a number of red-hot pointed irons, and they thrust them through his belly until they came out of his back. They did these things three times to him until his skin peeled off him. Afterwards the Duke said to him, 'Will you not now offer up sacrifice?' The Duke commanded his men to place hot ashes on his head and to put a helmet of iron on him. Aba Victor did not sink under this torture. The Duke made them take him off the frame of the rack and to lay him on the bed of iron, and to kindle a fire beneath it. He made them pour burning sulphur and pitch, mixed with other inflammable substances down his throat. The Duke said to Victor, 'Listen to me, and do not die a death of torture. Is it not better for you to be with me? Do you not wish to live with me?" Aba Victor was not able to answer a word because of the pain which he was suffering. The bed of iron was exceedingly hot under him.

The Duke said to Aba Victor, 'Speak one word to me, and I will release you, O you unholy exile!' Aba Victor said to the Duke, 'Seeing that I did not obey my father nor the Emperor when they made entreaty to me, and seeing that I continued my disobedience to the point that I forsook all my possessions, and abandoned this world which shall pass away, do you think that I will listen to you? It is written, "Man shall die, and the creeping things and the worms shall possess his inheritance," (Job 21:26) The Duke was angry, and he commanded his servants to throw Victor into the furnace of the public baths of Rakote, bound hand and foot. Again Victor bore iron fetters on his hands and feet and there was a gag in his mouth. Certain people of the city, both men and women and children, wept for him, and they said, 'Woe for this wretched man, for his body will be destroyed in the fire;

if only he had been one of those who offered up sacrifice!'

Aba Victor stood up and prayed in the midst of the fire, saying, 'I beseech You, O my Lord Jesus Christ, to be unto me a helper, and to assist me in all my tribulations, for I am a wretched and most miserable creature, in order that all this city may know that there is no other God besides You, Who alone are God.' At that very moment the holy Archangel Michael came down from heaven, and went into the furnace of the bath, spread out his holy apparel over Aba Victor, and he caused the flame of fire to become like dew at the first hour of the day. He lifted him up on his wing of light, and the wing turned into a green meadow.

Michael broke the iron fetters that were fastened upon Victor's hands and feet, and they both remained talking together concerning the mysteries of the kingdom of heaven, the city of the righteous.

After these things, the Duke said to those who were sitting with him, and to the men of Rakote, 'O Alexandrians, Jesus shall not deliver him out of my hands, for there are no gods besides Apollo and Artemis.' Aba Victor said to the Duke, 'O lawless man, why do you revile my God? You are wondering where your god Apollo is, and you say, "Offer up sacrifice to the gods who cannot move." Nevertheless you know well that there is power in my God to deliver me from your tortures.' Armenius, the Count said to him, 'This day I know that you are an arch magician, and that you work magic.' The Duke sentenced Aba Victor to be beheaded.

The magistrates and the people of Rakote entreated the Duke that he would not put Aba Victor to death in their city, because they were afraid lest Aba Victor's father destroy the whole city on account of it. The Duke meditated within himself, saying, 'What shall I gain by making his father an enemy of mine?' Then the Duke took a sheet of skin, and wrote on it the following words: "I, Armenius, the Duke of Rakote, write to Eutuchianus, the Count of Thebaïd. Examine the case of Victor carefully and either make him offer up sacrifice or put him to death, according to the decree of our Lord the Emperor." The Duke delivered Aba Victor over to the soldiers that they might take him to the south, to Thebaïd, to Eutuchianus, the Duke of Thebaïd.

VICTOR SENT TO EUTUCHIANUS, DUKE OF THEBAID

On the twentieth day of Pharmoute they banished the blessed man Aba Victor and four soldiers brought him to the south in ten days. There was a collar of iron about his neck, chains on his hands and ankle fetters on his legs. The torturing had made him weak and helpless. When the soldiers arrived at Antinoë they tied up the boat to the shore, and they found that the governor had departed for the south. They unfurled their sail, and set out for the south, and they overtook the Count of the Thebaïd as he was lying becalmed in midstream, for there was no wind. The soldiers brought Aba Victor into the lower part of the boat. Now Victor had neither eaten nor drunk for twelve days and they delivered him over to Eutuchianus, the Duke, and they gave him a supply of food according to what the Count of Rakote had commanded.

The Count Eutuchianus commanded them to tie up the boat to the shore, and to set up his seat of justice at that place. When the morning of the following day had come, they prepared for him a seat of justice there. Aba Victor passed the whole night in the lower part of the boat, blessing God and saying, 'Blessed are You, O King of all the ages the Father the Almighty, and Your only-begotten Son Jesus Christ, our Lord, Who has delivered me from every place they have taken me. Stand by me in the future, and be with me in the presence of this lawless man.'

Eutuchianus commanded his men to bring Aba Victor to the shore, and he said to him, 'You are Victor, the magician. Now, therefore, in what way will thou work magic? Show me, before I disgrace you, and you die.' Aba Victor answered and said to the Duke, 'I am not a magician, and I have not devoted myself to the doing of this kind of work. On the contrary, I am a servant of Christ Jesus, Who hath delivered me out of all my tribulations.' Eutuchianus said to him, "Come now and offer up sacrifice with the men who are here, so that it may be well with you.' Aba Victor answered and said, 'I am not at all afraid of men, and I will not offer up sacrifice, but I am afraid of my Lord Jesus Christ. For it is written, "Do not be afraid of those who can kill your bodies upon the earth, because there is nothing besides this which they can do to you. But fear Him Who has the power to destroy your souls and your bodies in Gehenna."' (Matt 10:28)

The Duke said to him, 'Have you come here to convert us by a homily which is vain? If you dare again utter words in my presence, I will make my servants tear out your tongue. Unless your father compels me to release you, I will not set you free. You are worthy of death, and death shall now be your portion.' The Duke commanded his servants to fasten the hands of Aba Victor and they cut out his tongue and cut off the outer parts of his lips. They brought out his necessary organs, and poured boiling oil on them, and he made them pierce them with iron borers. They drove red hot tools into Aba Victor's ears and he made them thrust red-hot tools under the nails of his feet and the skin of his head.

The Duke said to him, 'Will you offer sacrifice or not? If you will not I will put you to death with excruciating tortures.' The soldiers bought vessels filled with boiling bitumen, which they emptied down his throat. The Duke said to him, 'Will you offer sacrifice or not, or will you die by torture?' The blessed man Aba Victor said to the Duke, 'Woe to you, O Duke! You deny God for the sake of things which have been made by the hands of man, and you and your Emperors shall be punished with severe punishment.' Eutuchianus was angry and he took an oath by the life of the Emperor and by the lives of the gods, and he said to Aba Victor, 'Since you will not sacrifice, and since you have been put to shame on the rack, I must destroy you by banishment until you die.'

Epiphanius the recorder answered and said, 'Listen to me, and let me say this thing to you, O my Lord Count. Behold, there is a certain Camp very far away in the south that is deserted, and there is no man living in it. Behold, it is fifteen years since I became a soldier, and during that time I have never seen any one in it. Now, therefore, banish Aba Victor to that place, and keep him there until he dies.' The Count of the Thebaïd commanded that this should be done, and he passed sentence on him, saying, 'I, Eutuchianus, hereby command that this profane man Victor be taken to the Camp of Hierakion, and that he be compelled to remain there until he die.' Immediately four men seized Aba Victor and carried him away to that place.

VICTOR ENCOUNTERS THE DEVIL

The noble man Aba Victor was strong and of good courage, and he related to the four soldiers his sufferings up to that time. It came to pass on a certain day that Aba Victor was outside the place of torture and the Devil came to him in the form of a soldier, and said to him, 'Hail, Aba Victor. I am a soldier of the imperial Palace, and your father has sent me to give you this message: "Rise up, come back to me here, so that I may make you a General. Have I not suffered pain in longing for you? Come back, so that I may make you a General. Will you not listen to me? It is you yourself who has drawn upon your head these sufferings. Other people, strangers are eating up your goods." Do you not know that you are an only son, and that your parents have no son but you to succeed them? They have adopted one of their slaves and now he rides the horses, and the Emperor has made him a Count in your place. He wears your apparel, and meanwhile you are destroying your soul with tribulations. Behold, you art dwelling in this desert place! Are you not afraid lest thieves attack you by night?'

Then the Devil began to produce a written letter and he unrolled it before Aba Victor, and said to him, 'Look at this, and you will recognize the handwriting of your father and his seal.' Aba Victor looked closely at the man, and he knew that he was a phantom, and he said to him, 'Get away from me! It is through you that the whole world is in a state of disruption, and it is through you that the worship of idols flourishes.' The blessed man Aba Victor turned his face towards the east, and said, 'Show Your compassion upon me, O You only Son of Your Father, my Lord Jesus Christ, and deliver me out of all my tribulations.' When the Devil heard the Name of Jesus, immediately he made himself visible.

VICTOR MEETS JESUS CHRIST

Aba Victor continued to live in the Camp, and Jesus was with him in everything which he did. The noble man Victor meditated within himself and said, 'What kind of work can I do whereby I may live?' Now he had learned the trade of an artisan, and while he was living by himself in the Camp he used to make seats and lampstands. It came to pass one day while the blessed, man Aba Victor was living in exile that the Lord Jesus came to him. Now He had changed His apparel and had taken the appearance of a grey-headed old man, who had come from a far-distant place. He knocked at the gate of the Camp, and Aba Victor came outside, and when he saw the grey-headed old man he was filled with sorrow and compassion for Him, and he kissed Him, saying, 'Come inside, O my lord brother, You good man; it seems to me as if I had seen Jesus this day.' Aba Victor did not know who the old man was, and the two of them went into the tower in which Victor lived. Then Aba Victor said to the man, 'Let us offer up prayer to God'; and Jesus said to Him, 'Let us offer up prayer.' Aba Victor said to Him, 'You stand up first, because You are greater than I, and You are more holy than I. I am nineteen years old this day, and the sign of this world has not as yet ceased, to manifest itself in my body, and the wickedness of this world has not entirely disappeared from my heart.' Jesus said to him, 'Forgive me, O my brother! I will stand up and pray.' Jesus and Aba Victor spread out their hands, and it came to pass that as they were praying the ten fingers of Jesus became ten lamps of fire which penetrated to the throne of the Father.

It came to pass that when they had finished praying, Aba Victor went forward and saluted Jesus—now he did not know who He was—and he said to Him, 'Sit down so that I may be able to enjoy Your face fully, for behold, it has been a very long time since I have seen a man. I beg You to inform me truthfully of what place You are a native, so that I may know whether You are a native of my own city or not.' Jesus said to him, 'You are a Roman (Greek?) of Cilicia. Your father is Romanus, and your mother is Martha, and the wife whom they betrothed to you is Theonôè; but God has chosen you for Himself.' Aba Victor wept in His face, and said to Him, 'O my brother, great is Your faith. I see that You are a prophet, or perhaps You are an angel of God. Tell me news about my house for behold, it is a very long time since I departed from my country.' Jesus answered and said, 'O my brother, show an act of loving-kindness to me, and give me a cake of bread, so that I may eat it, for it is seven days since I ate food.' Aba Victor said to Him, 'In truth, O my brother, this day is the fortieth day in which nothing has entered my mouth, and for forty days I have not taken my clothes off my body. As the Lord lives, I have neither bread nor water in this wilderness, nor anything whatsoever which has the appearance of food. But now, O my brother, rise up, take this lampstand and these seats (or, stools), and also my shoe latchet, and go into the city which is near and sell them at their proper price, and buy us some bread that we may eat, lest our souls decay through weakness.'

Jesus answered and said to him, 'Where in this wilderness do you find a man with whom to converse? Who is it that takes care to provide you with food?' Aba Victor answered and said to Him, 'Woe to me, O my brother! Long will it be before I shall arrive in that other world in which no respect of persons is shown. May You find it. My Lord Christ dwells there, the Apostles and the Patriarchs dwell there, and thousands of thousands, and tens of thousands of tens of thousands stand round about it. If any man who is a sinner shall arrive there he shall not find boldness (or, freedom of speech) there, because of the sins that he has committed, both of those committed during the day and those committed during the night. As for me, how wretched shall I be in that hour! Woe is me, because of the ignorance which has been set in the hearts of men, whereby each one fails to remember death until the moment when it overtakes him before he knows it! Woe is me, for I have made supplication to death, but I have not found it. I have begged that some sickness might attack me, but it has not done so. You know, O my Lord, that I have made entreaty for my death more than for my life, for I am without father and without mother in this world. I bear witness by my Lord Jesus Christ, that if You depart from me this day, You shall come back again and shall visit me. I am the servant that is unprofitable. When I shall die You shall bury my body, lest it remain lying about in this world, in which there is no man whatsoever who shall remember me.'

Then Jesus had compassion on Aba Victor, and He looked upon him as he wept, and said to him, 'Do you know Who I am? I am He Who delivered you from the rack of torture at Rakote. I am He Who delivered you from the iron bed. I am

He Who kept you in safety in the furnace of the bath. I am Jesus Christ, Who delivered you from all your tribulations. I will be with you in every place wherever you shall go. Do not grieve because you are living in this wilderness. Truly, I say to you, that you shall be with Me in Jerusalem of heaven, My beloved city. As I take My seat upon My throne, you shall sit upon your throne. I will make every tyrant (or, governor) and every ruler to hold in wonder your name whenever they hear it. I will make them come to your shrine, and to bring gifts to you in My Name. I will make many mighty wonders and signs to become manifest at your shrine. The story of your life shall reach the uttermost ends of the earth. This year you shall dwell in exile, but in the next year they shall cut off your head with the sword; for you shall suffer certain pains for My Name's sake. I will come to you again, and I will give you strength.'

Immediately Aba Victor cast himself down at the feet of the Lord, saying, 'Who am I, that I should be deemed worthy by You for You to speak to, O my Lord?' Jesus kissed him and departed into heaven, and the angels sang hymns to Him. Aba Victor continued to live in the Camp, and the Lord Jesus was with him. He purchased for himself materials for his burial and his coffin. Large numbers of soldiers flocked to the Camp for the sake of the blessed man Aba Victor. He doubled the number of the prayers which he used to make, and he kept fasts for very long periods, and he diligently observed the Sabbaths, and the Lord Jesus was with him.

VICTOR CONTINUES TO DENY THE WORSHIP OF IDOLS

It came to pass that after Saint Aba Victor was banished, he lived in the Camp. Sebastianus, the Duke, came to inspect the Camp. Asterius, the praetor of the Camp, cast himself down before the Count, and Sotêrichos, who was the accountant, gave him a written statement concerning Aba Victor, so that he might summon him into his presence. Then the Duke ordered his servants to set his judgment throne inside the gate of the Camp, in order that he might hear the case of the holy man Aba Victor. When morning had come the Duke took his seat upon the throne, and he commanded his servants to bring the righteous man into his presence. The torturers seized Aba Victor while he was in his cell, and he had lentils in his hand, and he was eating, and Aba Victor threw the lentils through the window, saying, 'O my Lord Jesus Christ, make these lentils become stones which shall never be destroyed! They shall be a sign to all the generations which are to come, lest these wicked men tread them down.' Aba Victor prayed, saying, 'O my Lord Jesus Christ, let me not be put to shame before this wicked man.' Afterwards he came down from his cell, and stood before the Duke.

The Duke said to him, 'These are the letters which the Emperor has sent to be read to you; listen to them, and offer up sacrifice.' Aba Victor answered and said, 'I belong to a King Who is deathless, and therefore I will not worship an emperor who will die. For all the kingdoms of the world shall perish and be destroyed, but the glory of God shall never, never perish; therefore I will not offer up sacrifice. Truly, I know well that I received a salary of sixty from my father, who is a general, and that God hated me because I received these things wickedly. Now therefore, O Duke, neither gold nor silver will be of the least value to a man in the hour of his necessity. For this reason let us fight with ourselves, for forgetfulness has spread itself over our heart, so that we may never cease to remember the death that comes in this world. I have never glorified myself, and I have never exalted myself. For this reason that which is written is fulfilled in me: "He who exalts himself shall be abased, and he who abases himself shall be exalted."' (Matt 23:12)

Sebastianus was exceedingly angry, and he said to Aba Victor, 'Offer up sacrifice.' Aba Victor answered and said, 'I will not offer up sacrifice. Whatsoever you wish to do to me that do. I fell into the hands of the four torturers before this, and I was not afraid of them, for the Lord gave me strength during all my torturing. Now therefore, O Duke, I was banished to this spot because of this Name, for they said, "Offer up sacrifice," and I would not do so. Moreover, I do not wish to remain in this world that shall dissolve away and perish. Let it be known to you also, O Duke, that if you put me to the torture many, many times, you will only give additional strength to the reasoning power of the mind which is within me. Wholly fitting for me is it that I should be held worthy to endure reviling for the Name of the Christ.'

The Duke said to Aba Victor, 'Stop talking; you are always talking! Are you a deacon, or a reader, that you possess such perfect knowledge of this kind of wisdom?' Aba Victor said, 'I would give thanks to the Christ if I were, only I am not worthy of so great a gift as this—to be made a deacon or a reader. The grace of God is received through Jesus Christ, Who gives wisdom to every man whose heart is right with Him, because He is the giver of riches, and His treasury is filled with wisdom which He gives to every one who shall profit through Him in respect of good things. For as the good farmer is in the habit of giving manure to his field, so that he may supply it with strength and enable it to bring forth its crop, even so does the wisdom of God live in the soul of him that seeks after it, and it permits neither the net of death nor the wiles of the Devil to have dominion over it. For the Lord is mighty, and He is able to perform everything.' The Duke said to him, 'Do you then go so far as to choose for yourself death rather than life?' Aba Victor answered and said to him, 'This death is not by any means death, but life everlasting. I am able to endure patiently your torturing.'

The Duke made his servants strip Aba Victor naked, cut his tendons, fasten his hands behind him and to drive skewers into him. Afterwards he made them dissect him. The Duke said to him, 'Offer up sacrifice.' Aba Victor said to him, 'I will not offer up sacrifice.' He made his servants break the joints of his legs and arms until his bones stuck out through his skin. Aba Victor said to him, 'I give thanks to You, O my Lord Jesus Christ, because all the joy of Christ has drawn near to me.' The Duke said to him, 'They delivered you over into my hands as a magician. Now, then, if you do not obey me, I will torture you with the most terrible tortures.' Aba Victor said, 'I will not offer up sacrifice.' The Duke said to him, 'Why do you take no pleasure in your chariot and in your armour?' Aba Victor answered and said, 'They are used in acts of violence. For this reason I will not eat the rations. I have in the world which is to come spiritual food laid up for me, and when I have eaten of it I shall never feel hunger again.'

The Duke commanded them to strip him naked and to cast him into a furnace in which the fire had been lighted for two days. Afterwards they brought him into the presence of the Duke, who said to him, 'O wicked head! I swear by the health of Apollo that your punishment shall be the destruction of your body by fire.' The Duke commanded his servants to prepare a furnace, and to heat it for four days, and then to cast Aba Victor into it. Aba Victor prayed in the depths of the furnace, saying, 'O my Lord Jesus Christ, at the mention of Whose Name the sea dried up, let this fire be extinguished, and let the heat of it be destroyed. Blessed be Your Name for ever! Amen.'

VICTOR AND THE MAGICIAN

The soldiers brought him and set him before the Duke, and it was found that the fire had not touched him. Then Sebastianus said to Aba Victor, 'By the glorious gods Apollo and Artemis, I will torture you sorely, I will send and bring a magician who is more powerful than you, and he shall make an end of your magic.' The Duke commanded them to bring a magician. The magician came, and he made medicaments containing the essence and the venom of serpents, and he pronounced over them a very large number of magical names. After this, he said to Aba Victor, 'Take these, swallow them, and then I shall see if you are strong enough not to suffer from it.'

The blessed man Aba Victor said to the magician, 'I have no desire to swallow them, but in order that you may know that my God has power to make of no effect every kind of magic, I will do so.' Aba Victor made over himself the Sign of the Cross in the Name of the Father, the Son, and the Holy Spirit, saying, 'Do not let me be put to shame before this lawless man.' Afterwards Aba Victor swallowed the medicaments and he did not suffer the least of injury. On the contrary, he was filled with a feeling of happiness like the happiness of those who have been drinking wine. The magician made other medicaments that were far more powerful than those that he had made first, using even the gall and the humours of a corpse. These he placed in a vessel, and he pronounced over them such mighty magical names that even the earth shot out light at the mention of them. He said to Aba Victor, 'Take these this time also, and if no evil thing happens to you I will believe in your God.' Then the blessed man took these medicaments and drank them and no evil happened to him.

The magician said, 'Strong indeed is he who has shown strength! Mighty is he who has shown might! You have delivered your soul from death, and made it live once again.' Immediately the magician relinquished all the possessions that he had, and he was taught the Name of the Holy Trinity, and all his books that were full of magic, he burned in the fire.

VICTOR IS TORTURED AGAIN

The Duke said to Aba Victor, 'Be wise, and offer up sacrifice.' Aba Victor said to him, 'Indeed I am wise at all times.' The Duke said to him, 'But this time you are acting foolish.' Aba Victor said, 'The fools of the world are those whom God has chosen to put to shame the wise.' (1 Cor 1:27) The Duke said to him, 'Where is this writing found?' Aba Victor said, 'It is Paul who wrote it.' The Duke said, 'Is Paul then a god?' Aba Victor said to him, 'As the wise man, among architects, when he is about to build seeks for a site on which another has laid the foundation, and then builds upon it, even so is Paul, who came at the end—he sets the roof on the Scriptures.' The Duke said to him, 'Stop speaking such foolish words as these, for these actions will profit you nothing, and you shall die. You are a child. Listen to me now; offer up sacrifice so that I may set you at liberty.' Aba Victor said to him, 'I am not a fool; I am a wise man. If I were to obey you, and if I were to offer up sacrifice, I should in truth be a fool. Fools can never walk in the truth, because their hearts make them blind, and they become liars, like their father the Devil.'

The Duke was angry and he commanded his servants to tear out the intestines of Victor's body. Aba Victor spoke before the Duke, saying, 'The tendons, nerves, and sinews which you have dragged out from my body are like the pointed instruments with which the physicians probe a wound in order to liberate the foul pus which is in it, and to give relief to the whole body. That is the case with me at this moment. Now I will give thanks to my Lord Jesus Christ, forever and ever. Amen.'

The Duke made his servants bring some oil, and they lighted a fire under it, and kept it burning until the oil was boiling. He made them pour it upon his necessary organs. The blessed man Aba Victor answered and said, 'This oil which you have poured upon me is like cool water which a man drinks during the hot weather, and in which he washes himself so that he may feel relief by it from the heat in his whole body.' The Duke commanded his servants to hoist him up on the rack of torture, and to stretch him on it, and he made them put six burning torches close to his body; and they racked him for a period of two hours. The fire did not scorch his body in the least degree, for God was with him, and He gave him strength in all his tribulations.

The Duke said to him, 'O wicked head! I weary myself. I want to spare you from being put to shame, and you will not turn (i.e. repent). Come now, offer up sacrifice.' Aba Victor said to him, 'Yesterday you spared me; today do not spare me. Do whatever pleases you to do to me.' The Duke commanded his servants to pour vinegar and ashes into Victor's mouth. Aba Victor said, 'This vinegar and these ashes, which you make me drink, are like honey dropped down my throat.' Then the Duke commanded his servants to dig out his two eyes while he was alive. Straightway the executioners came and thrust red-hot knives into his eyes and ears, and instantly his two eyeballs were ripped out and fell on the ground. Dizziness mounted up in Victor's brain but Aba Victor said to the Duke,

'Even if you have the power and blind the eyes of my body, I have still left within me other eyes. That is to say, those of the mind and understanding, which will give me light, according to that which Peter the Apostle said, "If it be that you see with the eyes of the body, you shall see the works of the world, which are vain, that is to say, fornication, and slandering, and murder, and pride, because of which things the wrath of God comes." Therefore I have no need of the eyes of my body.'

The Duke answered and said to him, 'If you compel me now to inflict further severe tortures upon you, I must do so.' Aba Victor said to him, 'Inflict upon me any punishment you wish to inflict, for I am prepared to bear up under it; only take care not to spare me.' Then the Duke commanded his servants to hang him up on a pillar head downwards for three days and three nights, so that all his blood might pour out from his mouth and nostrils. The soldiers who had hung him up departed to their houses, and left him hanging. After three days the Duke commanded them to bring him down from the pillar so that he might know whether he was alive or dead. Straightway the soldiers departed to fetch him. When they laid their hands upon him, they became blind. Aba Victor said, 'In the Name of my God, for Whose sake I am suffering all these sufferings, receive your sight through His power, which is holy.' Immediately they received their sight. When the Duke saw what had taken place, he commanded the soldiers to flay his body and to tear out his tongue. Aba Victor said to the Duke, 'Even though you strip off me my skin which is outside me, I have still another skin, which is inside me, and which neither your power nor your tortures can injure. Again, though you shall cut out my tongue, God executes judgment on behalf of those whose mouths are silenced. Now, therefore, I care nothing for your tortures.'

VICTOR AND STEPHANOU

While the blessed man Aba Victor was saying these things, behold, a certain young woman whose name was Stephanou, who was the wife of a soldier, looked out through her window. Now she was about fifteen years of age and she cried out, saying, 'Blessed are you, O Aba Victor, and blessed are you in all your works. All your sacrifices have been received from your hands, even as the sacrifices of Abel. God shall show compassion upon you as He did upon Enoch, the scribe of righteousness. You are perfect and righteous in your generation as was Noah. You believe on God, as did Abraham. You lay your body on the altar as a sacrifice, as did Isaac. You manifest patient endurance, as did Jacob at the time when Esau pursued him when he was going to Laban. You are a man of wisdom and understanding, as was Daniel the Prophet. You have been instructed in divine things by your dreams like Joseph.

You have manifested patient endurance like Job, the man of God. The Enemy has been envious of you as he was of Isaiah the Prophet, whose body they sawed in two lengthwise with a wood saw. The fire has not touched you, even as the fire of Nebuchadnezzar did not touch the Three Holy Children. (Dan 3:27) You have given your heart to God, even as did David, the son of Jesse. Behold, I swear by your salvation, Aba Victor, that two crowns shall be sent down from heaven, being borne by twenty-four angels; one of these is for you, and the other shall be for me. Though like you I am a vessel of infirmity, I shall have an inheritance among the mighty ones.'

When the Duke heard this woman proclaiming these things, he commanded his soldiers to bring her to him. When they had brought her, the Duke said to her, 'How old are you that you dare to proclaim these violent words in such an impudent manner?' She said to him, 'I am fifteen years and eight months old.' The Duke said to her, 'How many years is it since you married your husband?' She said to him, 'Behold, one year and six months.'

The Duke answered and said to her, 'Offer up sacrifice now and do not die an evil death.' She said to him, 'I will not offer up sacrifice because I wish to receive the crown which is indicated by my name.' Then the Duke was exceedingly angry and he commanded his soldiers to set her between two palm-trees and to tie her to each of them. They pulled the trunks of the two palms close to her body by means of a rope and tied them together. Afterwards the two palms were released suddenly by cutting the rope and in this way she was torn apart down to the middle of her body and she became two pieces. Thus she fulfilled her martyrdom in peace and she departed into the heavens, to Him Whom she had loved, the Christ, in great glory. Amen.

VICTOR GETS BEHEADED

Then the Duke passed the sentence of death upon Aba Victor, and ordered his soldiers to cut off his head. The blessed man Aba Victor answered and said to him, 'I give thanks to my Lord Jesus Christ, Who has given me these riches for ever. Now, therefore, hear me, and I will declare to you the following things that have been revealed to me. Now after I am dead you yourselves shall also die, at the end of my eleventh year. Concerning the Duke Sebastianus, an ekstasis shall take place and certain men in a town shall delay in paying tribute, and he shall embark in his boat and depart to despoil them, and as the crew is tying up the boat to the bank, the Duke shall come forth. As he is coming down from the boat by the landing plank, he shall trip, and he shall die at the end of the twenty-fourth year after my death.

Again, all the wise men and all the speakers shall go and eat their midday meal together at the end of the eighth year after my death, and the house in which they are in shall fall down upon them, and they shall die together. When Asterius, the governor of the Camp, who delivered the written accusation of me to the Count, shall tie up his ass on the north side of the Camp, she shall bite him, and he shall fall ill and die. After ten days the men of my household shall come seeking my body; give it to them, for I have already bought the funerary shrouding for my body and my coffin. Only do not prevent my body from being given to those who shall seek after it. For there shall be an exceedingly great disturbance of the sea, and mighty events shall take place in the spot in which my body shall be deposited. The people of the whole country shall come to my shrine, and many mighty deeds shall take place on the spot where they shall deposit my head. The people of the whole country shall come to my shrine by reason of the mighty deeds that shall be done in it. I am a young man twenty years of age. I entreat you all, O my fellow soldiers, to let me depart to the presence of my Lord Jesus Christ. This is the day which I have been long expecting, and behold, it has come this day.'

Immediately they tied a gag in his mouth. Aba Victor said to the executioner, 'Dismiss me speedily, for the sake of the angels who have hold upon me.' Now the executioner was not pleased to do so, for he only struck his neck with the sword, and his head hung by the skin of the neck. Aba Victor was in torture and his spirit was sorely distressed in him. He looked up and saw a man called Horion the Kourson, and he said to him, 'Take the sword out of the hand of this lawless man, and make an end of me, for this wicked man of Assiut has already done very many evil things to me during my lifetime, and now also at my death he grievously afflicts my spirit. May the Lord reward him according to what he has done to me.' Horion the Kourson said to Aba Victor, 'My lord, do not think in your heart concerning me that I would lift up my hand against my brother soldier. I swear by your salvation, O my brother Aba Victor, and by the dire need which is on you, that I have never stretched out my hand even against a bird, to shed its blood, and it is impossible for me to lay my hand upon you with violence. I ask you to remember me in the place to which you depart.' Aba Victor answered and said, 'The Lord Jesus Christ shall show mercy to you, for in this very same year you shall die, and the Lord shall forgive you your sins. The enemy and the martyr shall come forth to you and I shall follow after them and shall sing hymns with them.'

Horion placed his napkin before his face. Aba Victor said to him, 'O my beloved brother, I entreat you most earnestly.' Horion then girded on the sword. The Camp was shaken three times then he cut off his head and consummated Victor's martyrdom. Horion lifted up his eyes to heaven and saw the soul of Aba Victor being saluted by the saints. When they had taken off the head of Aba Victor, blood mingled with milk came forth. He consummated his glorious martyrdom on the twenty-seventh day of the month Parmoute, at the tenth hour of the day. All the words which he spoke before his martyrdom came true.

Peace be upon every one who has suffered martyrdom for the Name of our Lord Jesus Christ, to Whom be glory, and to His Good Father, and to the Holy Spirit, life-giving and consubstantial, now and always, forever and ever. Amen.

THE ENCOMIUM OF CELESTINUS,
ARCHBISHOP OF ROME, ON ABA VICTOR

*The encomium which was pronounced by the glorious
patriarch, the authentic teacher, Aba Celestinus,
archbishop of the city of Rome, in honour of the martyr
and true crown-bearer in the Christ, the Holy martyr,
Saint Victor the general. He pronounced it on the day of
his holy commemoration, which is the twenty-seventh
day of the month Parmoute and he pronounced it in his
martyrium which the God-loving emperor had built for
him in Rome. He spoke also concerning the admonishing
of the soul which makes itself manifest in work, for there
is nothing certain in the life of man except suffering and
misery. He spoke concerning that which is written in*

the book of the apostle, 'It is a fearful thing to fall into the hands of God.' (Heb 10:31) He spoke concerning the miserable state of a man at the moment when he is about to yield up his spirit into the hands of God. Celestinus pronounced this encomium when the emperor Valentianus (sic) was present, and all his nobles, and all the people, both male and female, were with him, and they celebrated the glorious festival of Saint Victor, and marveled especially at the wisdom of Saint Celestinus. In the peace of God! May his holy blessing come upon us and may we obtain salvation! Amen. Bless us!

INTRODUCTION

He gives to His creatures food in its season, He opens His hand which is filled with righteousness of every kind and He makes the sky pour out rain at the time that is fitting. By these means the meadow becomes soft and bursts into flower, in order that all mankind may rejoice. He brings down upon the earth the rain in the season of rain, and the farmer cleaves the furrows of the meadow with the plough and casts the seed into them at the season of sowing. The grain begins to sprout and the plants that bear grain grow up and ripen, according to their kind. There is very great rejoicing in all beings, for they enjoy their food, and the things by which the body is sustained. Yes, even in the beasts of the field, which are accustomed to leap about and spring into the air when they eat the grass and herbs in the season of spring. The farmers rejoice exceedingly, because they have good hope of paying the revenue tax on their flocks and herds.

If now there is to be joy of this kind over the food that appertained to the body, how much greater should the joy be this day, O flock of reasoning sheep, O blessed Christian people, over the Blood that flowed out from the Side of God, and the Water that fell upon the earth? It made the world new again, and it became a fountain of water, which springs up unto everlasting life. All mankind rejoiced and leaped for joy, and they blossomed once again through the Water and the Blood that flowed forth out of the side of Emmanuel. They brought forth spiritual fruits, that is to say, the virtues of the Holy Spirit. There were some who chose for themselves purity from the time when they were born into the world to the time of their departure from it. There were others who had wives, and yet they were even as if they had had none. There were some who lived the lives of ascetics from the earliest years of their childhood to the last days of their old age, and fasted most rigidly. Some withdrew themselves from the world, and departed into the mountains, and became monks, and nobly fought the battle of the ascetic life to the day of their deaths. Others took up their crosses and followed after the Lord.

They poured out their blood in their confession of God, and they received the crown of martyrdom. In short, all mankind has blossomed and brought forth fruit with great gladness. The word that is written has been fulfilled in this generation, 'They shall all know You, from the least of them even to the greatest.' (Jer 31:34; Heb 8:11)

Our Saviour and His angels celebrate the festival of Aba Victor the General on the day of his commemoration, which is this day. All the ranks of the angels who are in heaven gather together and they ascribe glory to the man who withdrew himself from the world and its possessions. Christ loved him and crowned him with the crown of the kingdom which is in heaven. O Saint Victor the General! O you who wear the martyr's crown! O unconquered fighter! O true crown-bearer of Christ! O you who made your body a living sacrifice, holy and acceptable to God, I wish to pronounce an encomium upon you at your festival this day. Since my tongue is a tongue of flesh, and my heart (i.e. understanding) within me is that of a man, I am not able to describe adequately the glory and the honour with which God has invested you.

Among all the wise men who are in the world, who was there that was ever able to describe your honourable life completely, O Saint Victor? You were a virgin from your youngest days and an ascetic from your childhood. You fasted two days at a time during the whole period of your life. The door of your house was open to every one. For this reason I am afraid to set out upon the sea of your virtues; I know well the faultiness of my tongue, and that my heart has no wisdom in it. In what way is it possible for me to honour you according to what you deserve?

You were a virgin like Elijah and you never touched a woman. You were a righteous man, a man of good heart towards the poor, like Abraham the Patriarch. You were the martyr who was the mightiest of all the martyrs. You were not afraid of kings and dukes and governors, nor did tortures destroy your reasoning powers. The threats of your father Romanus did not prevent you from following your true Father, our Lord Jesus Christ. You held firmly upon the Rock which cannot be moved, Christ, until your last breath,

O you who were righteous in your generation, who made your body a sacrifice to God, what shall I say, or what shall I proclaim concerning you, O Saint Victor? I compare you to Noah, because you were perfect in your generation, as he was in his. I compare you to Abraham, because you were a lover of strangers, as he was. Now God and His angels sojourned with Abraham because of his love for strangers. (Gen 18:2) In your own case, O Saint Victor, it was the Christ Who came to you, and the Son of God was in the garb of a poor man. He comforted you in the Camp in a desert land, because of the great suffering which you had endured for His Holy Name's sake. I compare you to Isaac the Patriarch because his father took him to offer him up as a sacrifice to the Lord. (Gen 22:1)

In your case, however, O Saint Victor, by your own deliberate intent and choice you offered up your body as a whole burnt-offering to the Lord, through the manifold tortures which you suffered for the Name of Christ. I compare you to Jacob the Patriarch, because Christ took His name from him.

As for you, O Saint Victor, all the martyrs who are in the heavens boast themselves over you, and all the dwellers upon the earth do likewise, because of your patient endurance. I compare you to Joseph, because you fought against passion, even as he did. In the case of Joseph it was his brethren who sold him into slavery, but in your case, O Saint Victor, it was your father who delivered you over into the hands of the wicked. Joseph obtained a kingdom upon earth because of his patient endurance, but you, O Saint Victor, obtained a kingdom in the heavens. I compare you to Melchisedek and Aaron, because they offered up sheep and bulls as types (or, symbolically), while you, O Saint Victor, made your own body to be an offering to God. I compare you to Moses the Law-giver, because you yourself rejected the rank of General in this world and the riches of your parents and your own possessions and took up your Cross and followed your Lord.

Moses did not wish for men to call him the son of Pharaoh's daughter, but he chose to suffer with the people of God rather than to enjoy the pleasure of sin for a season. You also, O Saint Victor, did not wish for men to call you the son of Romanus, the first in the salutation of the Emperor. You rejected the honourable rank of General and your riches, and followed Him Who said, 'Whoever loves father or mother more than Me is not worthy of Me.' (Matt 10:37) You grasped the Generalship which endures forever.

I compare you with Isaiah the Prophet because you

yourself have seen Him that sits above the Cherubim and Seraphim and He came to you. He delivered you out of all your tribulation and gave you glory in the heavens and on the earth. He Who dwells in the heavens has made you a General among all the martyrs. Moreover, on the earth has He given you glory; glory so great that your sweet aroma has filled every country in the world. Men build martyriums to you in every place, in which mighty deeds and miracles take place. True is that which is written: 'Whoever shall ascribe glory to Me, him shall My Father honour.'

Your whole zeal was devoted to the love of God so God has graciously bestowed upon you the power of healing both the soul and the body. Although you heal the diseases of the body by means of the grace which God has given you, yet you also cleanse the diseases of the soul, which are sins, through the signs and the miracles which you make manifest in your martyrium in the four quarters of the world. O Saint Victor, your blood that has been shed has overthrown the pillar of Baal, even as Elijah did and you have destroyed its idols and pillars. (1 Kings 18:17) You have become the pillar of the whole choir of the martyrs. You have quenched the flame of fire by the power of God that is with you, like the Three Holy Children. (Dan 3:26)

What shall I say concerning you, O healer of the sicknesses that are secret as well as those that are manifest? He has even raised the dead by means of the oil of the sanctuary of his martyrium, in which you are assembled this day. I have seen the miracle with my own eyes, I the least of all here present. Now the Saviour said, 'Whoever believes in Me shall himself see the works which I do in the Name of My Father, and he shall do things which are even greater than they.' (John 14:12)

MIRACLES OF SAINT VICTOR

BIRTH OF A CHILD

There was in this city a certain man whose name was
Alexander, and he had great possessions in gold and silver.
This man had a wife who was barren, and who had never
given birth to a child. There was great sorrow in their hearts
because of this thing, for they had no heir to inherit their
substance. They heard of the mighty deeds and miracles
that took place in the martyrium of Saint Aba Victor, and
they rose up and went together to the holy shrine. They
made an offering in the martyrium on the Lord's Day and
afterwards they made a vow, saying, 'Hear this day in which

we supplicate to you. If you will come to us, and will give us the seed of man, we will dedicate him to your martyrium to the day of his death. Only take away the cause of the reproaches which we endure, and grant us our petition.' When they had said these things they departed to their house in gladness. It came to pass on a certain day that Saint Victor made supplication to Christ on their behalf, and the wife of Alexander gave birth to a male child, who was exceedingly beautiful to look upon. The grace of God enveloped him, and they called his name 'Victor', naming him after Saint Victor.

There was great joy in the house of Alexander and his wife, and they distributed much alms among the poor. When the child was five years of age the hearts of his parents would not permit them to send the child away to the shrine of Saint Aba Victor, according to the promise which had come forth from their mouths, but they went back on their vow. They did not remember that which is written, 'Take good heed to yourself to perform the words which come forth from your mouth, for the Lord will assuredly keep strict watch on your ways, and will take vengeance upon you.' Finally, the father of the child and his mother spoke together, saying, 'Behold, our hearts will not let us send the child into the shrine according to what we vowed. Let us call some man in the city who buys slaves, and let him put a value on the child, and we will give the value to the shrine, so that the martyr may not be angry with us.' They rose up and called a merchant in the city that bought slaves, and Alexander set before him all the slave children that he had on his estate. The merchant valued the child at forty holokotinoi. Alexander and his wife took the gold, and gave it to the shrine of the martyr, and they did not remember that it was written, 'If you shall vow a vow to the Lord you shall pay it.'

When Saint Victor saw that the parents of the child were not paying their vow in a right manner, and that they were thinking that the gift of God was like the other things which they could obtain by money, they were punished for their senseless behaviour. It came to pass on a day that the child was in the courtyard round about his father's house playing with a number of other children that a large stone dropped upon the child and killed him immediately. When his parents heard of this, they rent their garments and they cried out with a loud voice. They came rushing out with the servants, and they fell upon the child, who was dead. O what an exhibition of great grief was that which took place there at that moment! The parents cried out, 'Woe to us, beloved child! It is we ourselves who have been the cause of your death; because we made a vow, and we did not fulfill our vow. We dedicated you to the shrine of the holy man, and behold, he received you from our hands before you were conceived. He has burned up our bowels with grief for our beloved son. It is we who deserve death. What shall we do? At this moment we do not know.' The father of the child had a firm faith. He took up his little child in his arms, and the mother and his servants followed him. They brought him into the martyrium of Saint Victor and he laid him down before the altar of sacrifice. The father cried out, saying, 'O Saint Victor, I know that you have the power to do everything, and that it was you who graciously bestowed upon me this child. Do not act towards me according to my senseless behaviour, but consider graciously my tears, and make the soul of the child come back into him again, and he and we together will make ourselves slaves to you until the day of our death.'

When he had said these words, Alexander took a little oil from the lamp, and made the Sign of the Cross over the child and he put some on his lips and on his breast and on his belly. The miracle that took place immediately was greater than any miracle of Elijah and Elisha. At that very moment when the oil of the lamp touched the child (now what his father said was, 'May the skin of my hand make healing arise; return, O soul, into the child again') through the supplication of Saint Victor, the child opened his eyes. Great was the joy that fell upon his parents on that day. They cried out with a loud voice, saying, 'Great are You, O God of Saint Victor, and there is no god besides You in heaven or upon earth! In the place of grief You have given us gladness, and You have raised up to his parents the child who was dead.'

When the multitude saw the great miracle which had happened, they ran to where the child was and cried out, saying, 'One is the God of Saint Victor!' The father of the child went about the whole city with him and he clasped his hand and proclaimed the mighty deeds of Saint Victor. After this, he went into his house and brought out all his possessions and his slaves, and he gave them to the shrine of Saint Victor. The father remained in the shrine and served the Saint until the day of his death. The child became a man who was chosen by God. He lived a virgin all his life. He attained the rank of the presbytery and it used to be said of him that Saint Victor used to appear to him many times. True is the word which our Saviour spoke, 'Him who shall minister to Me shall My Father honour.' (John 12:26)

See, O my beloved, how exceedingly powerful is the

supplication of Saint Victor! Observe that God takes vengeance upon the man who makes a vow to Him and who does not pay it. As for us, when we make a vow to the martyr, let us fulfill it zealously in order that he may not be angry with us. Moreover, to vow and not to pay is a great sin. Take then good heed concerning that which you have vowed. However, we must not tarry in our discourse. Let us now go back and tell you concerning another very great miracle that took place in the martyrium of Saint Victor, to the glory of God and the martyr.

HEALING OF THE DEMON POSSESSED

There was in this city a certain woman whose name was Kallieutropia and she was the daughter of the sister of the Emperor Honorius. She was exceedingly rich. It came to pass one day, when she was lying down in her house, about the time of noon, in a cave-like place, at the hottest part of the day, that a certain demon leaped into her two breasts and hung down on her body. The woman was in very great torture by day and by night. She spent large sums of money on physicians, but obtained from them neither relief nor healing. She continued to suffer agonies and her husband fell into hopeless despair. The physicians used their utmost endeavors to work a cure upon her, the more so because she was a king's sister. However, they were powerless before the pain of the disease.

When the woman heard of the mighty deeds and miracles which were taking place in the shrine of Saint Victor, she made entreaty to her husband and to her brother that they would allow her to go to the shrine of the saint. Her kinsmen were persuaded by her, for they saw that she was in danger of dying. They commanded that a litter in which to carry her should be made ready, and they took her to the shrine of Saint Victor. When she had entered into the shrine, she cried out, saying, 'O my Lord Saint Victor, I entreat you to have compassion upon me, and to remove from me these pains which I suffer, for you are a saint of God.' In the middle of the night Saint Victor considered the misfortune of the woman, and he brought upon her a cessation of pain.

She lost consciousness as her slave and her eunuch were close to her. Saint Victor came to her in a vision. He was clothed in purple and he emitted rays of light, with a staff of light in his hand. He said to her, 'If you wish to be healed do this. When you rise up tomorrow morning take a little of the oil which is in the lamp that burns before the altar of sacrifice, and with it do smear your breasts, and the demon shall be painfully troubled, and shall come out of them. Take good heed that you do not display arrogance towards your slave-woman, and take good heed that you do not in future walk haughtily and stiff-neckedly. Take good heed to stretch out your hand to the poor. These sufferings have come upon you because of your uncharitableness and because of your pride.'

The woman became greatly disturbed and she answered with fright, 'Who are you, surrounded with such great glory?' He answered in a gentle voice, saying, 'I am Victor, the General of the Great King.' When he had said these words, she ceased to see him. Immediately she awoke from her dream and she smelled a very strong sweet smell that filled the whole martyrium. She said within herself, 'Truly this man who spoke to me was Saint Victor; I am a sinful woman.' Immediately she woke up her men, and told them her dream. When the morning had come, she went to the elder in the martyrium, and he gave her a little of the oil which was in the lamp. When she had taken it into her hand, she smeared her breasts with it, saying, 'In the Name of the God of Saint Victor, whose glory I have been held worthy to see; graciously grant me healing.' Immediately the demon became terrified and he leaped out of her breasts in the form of a gryphon.

All the people saw him and he was like a flame of fire. Immediately her breasts assumed their usual shape and she cried out, saying, 'One is the God of Saint Victor!' She gave splendid gifts to the martyrium, gold and very much silver, as a memorial of the healing which had taken place in her. Afterwards she went to her house to her kinsfolk, giving glory to God and to His holy martyr.

HEALING OF A WORKMAN'S FALL

Again it is necessary for us to tell you of another great miracle that took place through this holy man. It came to pass that when the Emperor Honorius saw the healing which had taken place in his sister, through Saint Victor, he rejoiced exceedingly. It pleased him to restore the apse of the altar chamber and to decorate the woodwork of the martyrium with fine gold, as a memorial of the glory of the saint. He caused handicraftsmen who were masters of their craft to be brought, and they began their work of decorating the chamber of the altar with gold. While they were working on the woodwork, the Devil, who hates that which is good, overturned one of the workmen while he was at work, and he fell to the ground.

The other workmen were afraid and they cried out, saying, 'Lord, have mercy upon us.' The Emperor and the other men who were below were greatly disturbed because of what had taken place. Behold, at the very moment when the workman began to fall, Saint Victor appeared from heaven, arrayed in great glory, and he laid hold of the hand of the workman before he reached the ground. When he was three cubits above the ground, St Victor held him suspended there. Then he went up with him to the woodwork, and set him down on his feet in front of the woodwork by the side of his fellow workmen. The workman had suffered no injury and no man had seen Saint Victor, with the exception of the workman.

When the Emperor and the multitude had seen the mighty miracle which had taken place, they were afraid, and they cried out, 'One is the God of Saint Victor, and besides Him there is no other god, either in heaven or on the earth.' When the workman had recovered from the attack of terror which had come upon him, he proclaimed to the Emperor and to all the people, saying, 'I saw a huge creature with his wings spread out, and his eyes were filled as it were with fire, and he struck me with what he had in his hand, and threw me down. While I was falling down, behold a man of light who was wearing the apparel worn by men of royal rank, and whose face was shining like the sun, laid hold of my hand before I could reach the earth: and he came up with me, and brought me into this place. He made the Sign of the Cross over me, and he removed fear from me, saying, "Do not be afraid, for I am Victor, on whose martyrium you are working." Immediately I ceased to see him.'

When the multitude had heard these things they cried out, saying, 'One is the God of Saint Victor!' Thus by the zeal of the God-loving Emperor and the might of Saint Victor, the decoration of the woodwork of the altar with fine gold and its inlaying with very costly stones were completed. Now, O my beloved, you see how great the mighty deeds and wonders of Saint Victor are, whose festival we are celebrating this day. To every man who shall make supplication to him with his whole heart, no matter what kind of sickness it is from which he is suffering, the saint will graciously bestow upon him healing.

HEALING AN INCURABLE DISEASE

Again there was a certain man in this city who was a patrician in the service of the Emperors. He fell ill of a certain kind of sickness that was incurable. His whole body swelled up to such a degree that he resembled a pillar. To see this man in such a state of wretchedness made one's heart ache, for he lived in great tribulation, and suffered excruciating pains. Often it would happen that you would find him sitting on the ground, and his servant would be obliged to carry him to his house. His feet and his other members would burst from time to time and eject large quantities of unclean matter. He gave a lot of money to the physicians, but gained no relief by it. Besides this, the Emperors of Rome sent the archiators to treat him, for he was a nobleman of high rank in the Palace. Yet he failed to find any relief whatsoever. Thus he continued to live, suffering these excruciating pains, until one day he heard of the mighty deeds and miracles which took place in the shrine of Saint Aba Victor. His servant lifted him up and carried him into the shrine of the holy man. He laid him down before the altar of sacrifice, and he cried out by day and by night,

'O Saint Victor, look upon my humility and my sufferings, and graciously bestow healing upon me, for I am grievously tortured. Let your mercy come to me, and make supplication to God on my behalf, so that He may take me out of this life of suffering. Behold, you see my tribulation by day and by night.'

He lost consciousness for a short space of time. Behold, Saint Victor gave consideration to his miserable condition, for he is a lover of mankind. The sick man saw him in a dream, appareled in great glory, wearing rich purple garments, girded with a girdle of gold and he shot forth from his person rays of light. Aba Victor said to the sick man in the dream, 'Why are you here in this condition?' The sick man said to him, 'Behold, you see my sufferings and my tribulations, and that I have drawn near to death.' The holy man said to him with a joyful face, 'I am he who shall cure you, for you must know that I have the power to do everything through the grace of God which is with me.' He stretched out the rod which was in his hand, and he laid it upon the sick man, saying, 'Healing shall come to you this day. Do not sin again, or evil which is worse than this shall befall you; and do not show yourself haughty towards the poor.'

The sick man answered and said with trepidation, 'My lord, who are you that appear in this form? I have never before seen any one like you, whether it be Emperor or whether it be General in the Palace.' He answered and said to the man, 'I am Victor, the General of the King of heaven.' When he had said these things to him, the man ceased to feel pain, and he ejected a mass of pus, which was so abundant that it overflowed and soaked all his bed. He ceased to swell up and became like a man who had never suffered from any skin disease at all. He leaped up on his feet, stood up, and cried out, saying, 'One is the God of Saint Victor!' When the multitudes who were gathered together inside the martyrium saw the great miracle which had been done, they cried out, saying, 'Blessed are we, because we are held to be worthy to have this pearl in our city, for he heals our sicknesses and our diseases.' The man gave gifts to the shrine of Saint Victor, both gold and silver, so that they might be distributed among the poor and the destitute. He departed to his house ascribing glory to God, and he took care for his soul till the day of his death.

What can I say about the miracles which you have performed, O wearer of the crown of Christ? What tongue of flesh is there that is able to describe your blessed estate, O valiant General? Truly, if I were to pass the whole of my time in going through the miracles that you have done, I should be wholly unable to recount even a small portion of them. O confessor and invincible athlete, who is there that is able to comprehend the full extent of your honourable estate, and the wonderful things that have taken place in your martyrium? For as it is impossible for a man to estimate the honourableness of this holy man, so also is it impossible to declare the mighty deeds which have gone forth from his sanctuary. O you who despised a kingdom in this world in order that you might receive one that was more excellent and belonged to heaven, great is the glory which God has given you both in heaven and upon the earth!

As I have already said, the sweet odour of you has filled all the countries of the world and men make mention of your name in every country, from the Camp in which you completed your course even to the region of the First Cataract. They ascribe glory to you throughout the world, saying that you are the greatest of the martyrs. The wonders of healing exist for those who shall believe on your name, and this very same gift comes forth from your martyrium and goes from one end of the inhabited world to the other.

HEALING OF A KALKYNWMA (TUMOUR)

It came to pass that when the God-loving Emperor Constantine built this martyrium, in which we are assembled this day in honour of Saint Aba Victor, that a certain great General fell sick of a very severe disease. Now he was sixty years of age and he suffered great pain in his inward parts. He was unable to sleep and he was sick with the disease that the physicians call kalkynwma. He had given large sums of money to one physician after the other, without feeling any benefit from their treatment. On the contrary, he was in imminent danger of dying. He heard about the mighty deeds and miracles which took place in the martyrium of Saint Victor in Antioch, and he rose up and went to Antioch. He passed two days in the martyrium and did not receive healing.

On the night of the third day, he felt a slight alleviation of the pain through the invincible power of God and immediately Saint Victor came to him in a dream. He was in the form of a mighty General and his face shot forth rays of light. He said to the sick General, 'If you wish to be made free of this disease, rise up quickly and depart to the martyrium of Saint Victor which is in Rome. You shall drink the water that is in the vessel in the chamber of the altar of sacrifice, and you shall find healing. Was it because my martyrium, which is in Rome is difficult to reach that you came to this place? Did you not know that my power is in all the world, and that it is the very same gift of healing which is to be obtained in them all, by those who believe and do not falter between two opinions? Did you not know that this very same power permeates my martyrium that is in Rome and that which is in Antioch? Why did you bring upon your head the distressing trouble of journeying over a sea of ocean to come to this place? Did you not know that I have the power to heal in this place? I will not do this in this place, and unless you go to my martyrium which is in Rome you shall not find healing.'

The sick General trembling answered and said, 'My lord, who are you who appear in this form and are surrounded with such great glory?' Aba Victor answered and said, 'I am Victor the General. I will heal your body. I will give salvation to your soul.' Immediately the sick General awoke from his dream and he was trembling exceedingly. He said, Truly this is Saint Victor, who has come to visit me.' Immediately his heart trembled, and he said, 'Forgive me, O my lord Saint Victor, because I was careless about going to your shrine which has been but recently built in my city, and came to this place.' He awoke his servants and told them about the dream which he had seen; and then he gave great and splendid gifts to the martyrium which is in Antioch.

After this, he went up into a ship and came to the city of Rome. He went into the martyrium of Saint Victor and he lay down to sleep, being in great tribulation. He supplicated to God and to the holy martyr, saying, 'O my lord Saint Victor, who considered me to be worthy of the sight of your glory in your martyrium, which is in Antioch, who commanded me to come to this place, I believe, O my lord, that your power goes through the whole world. Let your mercy come upon me, and graciously grant healing to me, for I am suffering very greatly.' When he had said these things, he lay down until the evening.

Afterwards he made them bring to him a little water in the vessel from the altar, and he drank it, even as Saint Victor had told him to do. Immediately the God of Saint Victor brought to him a cessation of the pain and contrary to his usual custom, he slept through the whole night. At the hour of dawn, the martyr came to him with great glory and said to him, 'Do you know me?' The nobleman said to him, 'Yes, my lord, I know you. You are Saint Victor. It was you who appeared to me in your martyrium at Antioch, and you sent me to this place.' The saint said to him, 'Have I not already told you that my might fills every place, and that it is the very same power which abides continually in all my martyriums, from one end of the earth to the other, and which heals every one who shall believe in me without doubt or hesitation? Have you never heard that which is written, "Everything is possible to him that believes?"' (Mark 9:23) The man answered and said to the saint, 'I do believe, my lord, that your power fills every place, but having heard concerning the mighty deeds which took place in your martyrium which is in Antioch, I went there to seek healing for my body.' The saint said to him, 'As it is with my martyrium which is in Antioch, so is it with that which is in Rome, and so is it with all the churches in the earth which have been built in my name, from one end of it to the other. My strength shall work in them to the very end of this age for him that shall believe in me. I will heal all diseases, both those that are secret and those that are manifest, through the gracious gift that God has given to me. Now, therefore, behold I will bestow upon you the gift of health of the body, but you must pray at the same time for the health of your soul, so that no evil may arise for you from this cause.'

When Saint Aba Victor had said these things to the man he hid himself from him. The man woke up in the morning, and he found that the diseased portion of his inward parts, that is to say, the hard ulcer had burst, and he vomited from his month a very large quantity of pus. He became immediately just like one who was not diseased at all. He sent abroad the report of the things that Saint Victor had said to him throughout the whole city. From that day onwards the saint granted the gift of healing to every sick person who went into his shrine. The man gave great gifts to the shrine of Saint Victor and he went to his house, giving glory to God. In all his troubles he besought Saint Victor to be his helper and he fasted and prayed until the day of his death.

You see, O my beloved, how very great and mighty are the miracles of this holy man whose festival we are keeping this day. As for us, let us believe with all our hearts on the mighty works and miracles of this holy man, in order that he may make supplication on our behalf to God. For whoever disbelieves in the mighty works of the saint, not only shall they be of no benefit to him, but his unbelief shall be to him a source of condemnation. However, let us not waste words, but let us return to our subject and describe to you the following great miracle which took place in the shrine of Saint Aba Victor, to the glory of God and His saint

.

HEALING OF LEPROSY AND BLINDNESS

There was a man in this city whose name was Anastasius and he was exceedingly rich as he belonged to a noble family. When this man had become very old in days, one hundred years old, he became sick of the disease which the physicians call elephantiasis. His whole body dried up and he became leprous, as white as snow. Many times he felt shame before the men who looked upon him for his body became covered with patches like that of a leopard. He was exceedingly grieved in heart over this matter because he was ashamed to go into the Palace. After these things, God put it into his heart to go to the martyrium of Saint Aba Victor, and to pray to him so that he might cure him of his disease altogether. He used to see people who were suffering from various kinds of disease and whenever they went into his martyrium they obtained healing. In this way then Anastasius rose up in faith, and he went into the shrine of Saint Aba Victor with his servants and with very many possessions. He passed two days in the holy place making supplication to Saint Victor and he said, 'O Saint Victor, I believe with my whole heart that you are able to heal me of this leprosy. Help me, I pray, for I am ashamed, by reason of that which has come upon me, to let men look at me.'

While he was passing these two days in the martyrium, behold there came a man who had phlegm in his eyes. Through the great quantity of granulation which covered them, a white film had appeared in his eyes and he had ceased to see anything by means of his own sight. All the money that he had, he had spent on physicians, yet he remained wholly uncured. Finally, when he heard about the mighty deeds of Saint Victor, he made some men carry him into the martyrium and he lay on a bed next to the leper. He entreated the God of Saint Victor, saying, 'O my lord the General, have mercy upon me, and graciously bestow upon me the gift of light for my eyes.' That night God, Who listens to every one that cries out to Him in truth, was pleased to heal the two men at the same time through the intercession of Saint Victor, who does such miracles and mighty deeds as these.

It came to pass during that night, when the man who had the skin disease had eaten with his servants, and had lain down to sleep, that Saint Victor had compassion on the miserable state of the man with the skin disease and on the blind man, and he was pleased to make manifest his miracles. He came to the man with the skin disease, arrayed in great glory, and his face shone brightly, and he said to him, 'Do you know who I am?' The man answered, 'No, I do not, my lord.' The saint said to him, 'I am Victor, to whom you made supplication this day. I am the father of the martyrium. Now, therefore, if you wish to be cleansed from your skin disease, you shall rise up early in the morning, and shall take hold of the hand of this blind man who is sleeping by your side, and you shall lead him down to the pool of water which is by the door of the martyrium, and the two of you shall dip yourselves in it three times, in the Name of the Father, the Son, and the Holy Spirit. Then you shall see my power; your skin disease shall cease from you, and the blind man shall see. Only take good heed not to be careless in respect of what has been said to you, and you shall be made whole.' When Saint Victor had said these things to the man with the skin disease, he came forth from him. Immediately the man awoke from his dream and he was in a confused and agitated state. He smelt a very strong sweet smell round his bed and it was like the smell of the finest perfumed incense. He said within himself, 'Truly this man who came to me was Saint Victor, and he came to bestow upon me graciously the gift of being made whole.' He rejoiced exceedingly and blessed God. He shut up the matter in his heart, saying, 'I will tell no one about the vision'; and he waited to see the end of the matter.

When the light became stronger, the man with the skin disease said to the blind man, 'Perhaps you will get up, then we will go down to the pool and wash ourselves, for I believe by God and by His holy martyr, that if we do, He will graciously bestow upon us healing.' The blind man said to the man with the skin disease, 'Whatever you wish to do, that do, but I cannot do this. Behold, you know the pain and tribulation that I endure. The truth is that I am afraid to wash for the physicians ordered me not to allow water to touch my head.' The man with the skin disease said to the blind man, 'Get up, let us go and wash. God has the power to remember us, and He will bestow healing upon us.' The blind man was persuaded by these words. The man with the skin disease took hold of his hand in the midst of the whole multitude, and they went down to the lake. Having filled a large washing bowl at the place for drawing water there, they dipped themselves in it three times, saying, 'In the Name of the Father, the Son, and the Holy Spirit, and of the holy martyr. Saint Victor.' Immediately the man with the skin disease gained relief and his flesh became like that of a child. As for the blind man, the white film that was in his eyes burst and fell down into the water and his sight was completely restored.

They cried out, saying, 'One is the God of Saint Victor, Who heals every one by His holy power.' The multitudes who were gathered together in the martyrium, having heard what had happened, rushed outside at once to see the great wonders which had taken place. They cried out, saying, 'Great are the mighty deeds of God and Saint Victor. Great is the favour which God has worked for us, in holding us to be worthy to have your martyrium in our city.' The man who had had the skin disease declared to them everything, and told them how Saint Victor had spoken to him in a dream. The report of this miracle filled every place and I myself saw it with my own eyes.

The man who had had the skin disease, and the blind man, both of whom had been healed by Saint Victor, remained in his martyrium and ministered there until the day of their death. They gave diligent attention to the welfare of their souls. As for the lake in which they had washed, many mighty works of God continued to take place in it and they do so to this very day. So great a means of healing is it that any man who is sick, whether he be sick of the palsy, or whether he be possessed of a devil, in short, if he be suffering from any kind of sickness, immediately that he has bathed in that lake, he finds healing. These people go to their houses glorifying the God of Saint Victor. What shall I say about the things that you have performed by your righteous actions? You suffered greatly for the name of the Christ, O noble man, Aba Victor! Great is the glory that God gave to you in heaven and on the earth. Truly the word, which is written, is fulfilled, 'The sufferings of a time are not worthy of the glory which shall be revealed to us.' (Rom 8:18) Great is the glory which God has given to you, O holy General! So great is it that to every man who calls upon God in your name, the help of God comes speedily. This continues to be so even to this day, for He delivers every man who makes supplication to Him with his whole heart from dangers of every kind. If you do not believe this, listen and I will show you that it is indeed so.

VICTOR PROTECTS THE COUNTRY

It came to pass that when the barbarians, who are called Saban, rose up against the country of 'Romania', they were as many as the sands of the sea. They captured the frontier of 'Romania', and then they prepared a large fleet of ships to transport them from 'Romania' to our country. All those men who were of senatorial rank, all the common folk of Rome and all those who were in the immediate districts, gathered themselves together, and they celebrated the 'Catholic Synaxis' in the shrine of Saint Victor. The God-loving Emperor was there with the soldiers of his army.

Now it was the festival of Saint Victor, and my Father Innocent also was there with his clergy. When they had begun to recite the Communion Service with great solemnity and reverence, behold, certain letters which had been sent by the hand of the captain of the lightly armed skirmishing troops, who was called Roumentros, who had been sent by the eparch of the frontier of 'Romania', were delivered to the Emperor. They contained the following message: 'Hastily, prepare the army, and come to us quickly, and help us, for behold the barbarians have captured the frontier of Armenia (sic).'

The Emperor was much disturbed… but his hope was fixed upon God. When he had read the dispatch, immediately he wrote to the eparch, saying, 'Do not fear, I will come tomorrow in the morning, and all the Roman people with me.' When the captain (veletarius) received the dispatch, he departed. The Emperor and all the people were gathered together into the shrine of Saint Victor, together with the Archbishop and all the clergy, and they cast themselves down before the altar of sacrifice, saying, 'O Saint Victor the General, supplicate to God on our behalf, so that He may protect our country, and so that the godless barbarians may not have dominion over it.' They celebrated the great 'Catholic Synaxis' with great dedication until the tenth hour of the day. When the service was ended and the Archbishop had pronounced the benediction of peace over the people, they were about to depart to their homes, behold, there arrived another great captain (veletarius) who had been sent to the Emperor with another dispatch. Now it contained glad tidings, and there was written in it the following: 'Peace be to you, O God-loving Emperor! Be strong, and of good courage, for God has fought for you. Behold, the godless barbarians who revolted against your sovereignty, God has destroyed with their own swords. Each one of them has risen up against his neighbour, beginning at the second hour of this day, and they slew each other, and there is not one of them left; on the contrary, all are dead. Behold, all their harness and trappings and their horses we have sent to your majesty. Therefore do not trouble yourself, and do not let your mind be disturbed, O honour of the soldiers, for it is God who fights on our behalf with you.'

When the Emperor had taken this letter in his hand, he read it out to the congregation before they departed. They rejoiced exceedingly, and were very glad, and they knew immediately that it was Saint Victor the General who had destroyed the barbarians. Now they had begun to supplicate to him at the second hour of the day. They all cried out with a loud voice, and they ascribed glory to the God of Saint Victor, and the barbarians have never again attempted to invade 'Romania' to this day.

Conclusion

You see, O my beloved, that the power of the holy General, whose festival we are celebrating this day, is great. Let us cease from every work which is evil, all violence, all irregular behaviour and all guileful deeds which we are in the habit of committing, and let us make ourselves sons of his. Let us remember the sufferings which our Lord suffered for us and His holy martyrs. Let us bring forth fruit to God according to what is fitting, each one according to his power; one in purity, another in prayer, another in patient endurance and another in longsuffering. In short, let us never pass a moment without bearing fruit so that we may become a well-cultivated field of God. Let us spread abroad the fruits of righteousness. Hear the wise man Paul the Apostle who says, 'I beseech you, by the mercy of God, that you present your bodies a sacrifice, living, holy, and acceptable to God.' (Rom 12:1)

How, and in what way, shall we present our bodies, O Saint Victor, unless we guard our bodies and our hearts against all kinds of deceit, and all kinds of fornication. It is written, 'Without purity, no man shall see God.' Let us watch our tongues so that they do not speak slanderous gossip, and do not blaspheme, and do not utter words of immorality and ridicule. You shall teach your hands to pray, and shall keep them from acts of theft and violence, and you shall guard your feet from wandering from the door of the house of God. You shall watch your eyes so that they do not lust, and do not give a cause for offence in the part of the church where the women are. When you do all these things, it shall happen that you are presenting your body to God as a sacrifice. Hear the Prince of the Apostles, Peter, who says, 'I beseech you, O my brethren, as strangers and sojourners to abstain from fleshly lusts which war against the things in the soul.' (1 Pet 2:11) Now are we not, O my beloved, mere sojourners upon the earth? Does not a man walk like a phantom? He gathers together, but he does not know for whom he gathers.

Since we are indeed strangers and sojourners upon the earth, it is fitting for us to remember our everlasting habitation, which is to say, the Kingdom of God, into which, if we keep the commandment which has been given to us, we shall enter happily. Inasmuch as when we come into the world we weep, so also when we depart, we weep. Man is born with suffering and departs with suffering. There is nothing which rules the life of a man except misery and sorrow. Have you not heard that which is written, 'Let not your heart be heavy through satiety, and drunkenness, and the anxieties of life, because that day shall come upon you like a snare; for it shall come upon every one who dwells upon the face of the earth'? That day shall come upon everyone, whether he is king, or governor, or rich man, or poor man. No man whatsoever shall escape from that awful necessity, which is full of fear. Again, have you not heard that which is written, 'Possessions shall profit nothing in the day of wrath; it is righteousness only that delivers a man from death'?

Do not set your affections on worldly possessions, or on the pomp of riches. Do not bind your soul to dominion and power, or to gold or silver, for all these things become fetters to you. Possessions have no quality but sins will precede us and will take their stand at the throne of God. Have you never heard what our Lord spoke, 'Watch, for you know neither the day nor the hour'? Let us therefore watch by day and by night so that we may not let our bodies be without God for one moment.

Moreover, we do not know when they will seek after us. Let us not bind ourselves to the phantoms of wealth, for you do not know when it shall be demanded from you. Have you not heard what is written, 'A man shall not redeem a man, and a brother shall not release a brother; he shall not give himself to God in exchange for him as the price of the redemption of his soul'? This informs us that a righteous father cannot obtain the release of a sinful son, nor a rich brother obtain the release of a poor brother, nor a righteous son obtain the release of a sinful father; but every man shall receive according to what he has done.

Now therefore, O my beloved, distribute your riches and possessions in alms and oblations to the poor, in order that you may obtain the happiness which shall be without end. Do not put your confidence in the riches of this world and do not place any reliance on gold or on silver. Have you never heard Solomon, who says, 'I hate all the labour for which I had suffered under the sun, because I am obliged to leave it to the man who shall come after me.'? (Eccles 2:18) You fool, where do you obtain the knowledge that your son shall live after you and inherit your possessions, or that he shall live a long time and spend them all? Shall not God take care of your son without your help? Is it not God Who brought you up, and shall He not also bring up your son?

God has graciously given you the large amount of wealth which you have in order that you may rest and enjoy yourself in this world and in the next. Satan has shut your heart and does not allow you to be generous towards the poor; because of this you shall receive great and never-ending punishments. We see many rich men gathering together possessions with great toil and suffering. Merchants building large houses for themselves, [collecting] possessions and substance in abundance, gardens, and fields, large numbers of cattle, great quantities of household stuff and large sums of money, and they say that they are laying up a store for their children. Whilst they have such thoughts, their children are snatched out of their hands while they are babies, and strangers reap the benefit of their labours. They themselves depart to the throne of God being naked.

Do not say in your blindness of heart, 'When I am about to go forth from the body, I will write my will so that my children and my kinsfolk may give alms on behalf of my soul.' O senseless one, you very great fool, do you not know that when you go forth from the body, you will not even be like the man who is lord of one obolus? Moreover, no man will ever remember you again. You will not have the money that you have heaped up. You will not have the storeroom that is full of grain. You will not have your vineyards. You will not have the houses that you have built. No, you will be a stranger to them all. They will have ceased to be yours and will become things that belong to others. If they wish they would give to you; if they wish not they would not give to you.

Have you never heard the holy man Job, saying, 'When I came out of my mother's womb I was naked, and I will depart naked.' (Job 1:21) Likewise, the Apostle cries out, saying, 'We brought nothing with us into this world, and we shall take nothing with us when we depart.' (1 Tim 6:7) David says, 'When their spirit comes out of them they return to their earth.' (Ps 104:29; 146:4) O wretched man, how and in what way are you benefited by all these cares and all these anxieties? Now, you know the place where you were born, but you do not know the place where you will die. You know how many years you have lived up to this present time, but you have no knowledge of how many you have yet to live. You know in what way your parents who begat you died, but you do not know in what manner you will die.

Now, therefore, O man, take advice, and let my counsel

be pleasing to you. Redeem your sins by charity and your lawlessness by gifts of alms to the poor that you may have enjoyment in the riches that do not come to an end. Send gifts before you go forth from the body, so that you may depart to meet Christ with joy. When a man is about to meet a king of this world, he sends gifts so that the king may receive him. How much more is it meet for us to send gifts and alms to the King of the Universe? Solomon said, 'Cast all your possessions before you. Give alms as you have the power. Do not say, I have nothing to give.' Remember the poor widow woman who cast the two mites into the treasury? Christ justified her, saying, 'She has given all her means of living.' (Luke 21:4) Again He said, 'Whosoever shall give one of these little ones a cup of cold water in the name of a disciple, Amen I say to you, that he shall in no way lose his wage.' (Matt 10:42; Mark 9:41)

Do not be careless of your salvation because of the material things of this life, for they will not assist us in this world to the end. There is a worse evil that can be, namely, when we have come forth from this world, we may become as if we had never entered into it. Remember the hour in which the sickness of death shall come upon you. You shall cast yourself down on your bed, and you shall say, 'I am sick this day.' After a very short interval, the sickness shall become more severe on you, and a violent fever shall lay hold upon the wretched flesh of your body. Such excruciating pains and sufferings shall seize you that your normal condition of mind and body shall be disturbed. Your tongue shall shrink to nothing in your throat, your words shall dwindle in your mouth, your throat shall close up and no nourishment whatsoever shall be able to pass through it. The light in your eyes shall become less and less, and the sweat shall break out and cover your face. Great and bitter bile shall fill your body and the treatment of your eyes by the physician shall cease to be effective. You shall ask those who come to visit you, saying, "What time is it?" for your perception of things shall cease within you. Darkness and mistiness shall cover your eyes, and your face shall change its colour and become greenish-grey. Your hair shall perish, and the veins, tendons and sinews of your hands and feet shall dry up. Your heart and soul shall lose their strength by imperceptible degrees. O how terrible is this tribulation which is the greatest of all tribulations, and which is more fearful than death itself! Finally they will take your soul and will set it before the awful throne of God, and it shall receive according to what it has done, whether good or evil.

O Paul, wise man of the Apostles, your words are exceedingly sweet! When all men whom God has created shall go forth from the body, their souls shall be taken and shall be set before the throne of God. They shall do homage to the Righteous Judge and He shall pass sentence upon them before they are removed to the places of which they are worthy. Again, in the Day of the Resurrection, their souls shall rise, not having suffered destruction. The soul of every one shall return to his body and they shall receive according to what they have done, whether good or evil. We shall be examined and questioned concerning everything that we have done in this place of sojourning, even to the slightest word that we have uttered in jest. We shall be questioned, moreover, concerning the thoughts which have passed through our hearts. Christ spoke, saying, 'Let not any light, silly speech issue from your mouths, for you shall be obliged to give an account concerning them in the Day of the Judgment.' (Matt 12:36)

Blessed shall they be who shall rise up in the Resurrection of Life, for they shall reign as kings with Christ! Woe to those who shall be condemned to die a second time because of their evil deeds! When the Righteous Judge has ascended the throne, what He has brought shall be reckoned up. The tares shall be burned up in the fire that cannot be extinguished, but the wheat shall be gathered together into His granary, that is to say, into the kingdom that is in the heavens.

Therefore, let us turn ourselves and let us repent of our sins before inquisition shall be made concerning them. Remember that it is a fearful thing to fall into the hands of the living God (Heb 10:31). Show me what these pains and sufferings are worth. Man is absolutely a thing of naught. He is a man today, tomorrow he is dust and ashes. Man is a creature who eats and drinks this day, but tomorrow his mouth is closed. He who eats at this moment and who bathes in the bath, and who anoints himself this day with sweet-smelling ointments of the finest quality, is tomorrow rolled into the tomb. He who today sleeps on the roof (or, verandah) of his house clothed in garments of byssus is tomorrow cast forth into the tomb among the dead animals.

O miserable man, eating and drinking shall not deliver you this day. Why will not the possessions of riches deliver you? Why will not the phantoms of riches deliver you from these great necessities? Have you never heard about this foolish rich man, who was like yourself, and who said within himself, 'You have many good things laid up for you for very many years to come; take your ease, eat, drink, make merry?' (Luke 12:19) He thought that he would pass a very long time upon the earth. The sentence of God came upon him immediately, saying, 'You fool, your soul shall be taken away from you this very night, and these things which you have prepared, to whom shall they belong?' This is the case of every one who gathers in, and who is not a rich man in God. How then, O fool, are not your granaries, which are filled fully, unable to deliver you this day? Why do not your garments made wholly of silk and byssus deliver you this day? Have you never heard the words that David spoke, 'They shall leave their riches to others, and their tombs shall be their houses forever.' (Ps 49 10-11) The wise man Solomon spoke, saying,

'Leave all your property behind you, for there is neither knowledge nor understanding in Amente (Eccles 9:10), the place to which you shall depart.' That is to say, 'When you shall go forth from this world, you will not have the power to order anything rightly, no, those things which you would take with you are the very things on account of which you shall be judged.' Show me therefore, O fool, what all these pains and all these sins are worth, for you add sin to sin, and lawlessness to lawlessness, and guile to guile, and strife to strife. Do you not remember that which is written, 'The judgment is merciless for the man who has not shown mercy,' (James 2:13) and 'Remember that man is like a shadow, and that he brings his days to a close very speedily'? (Ps 144:4)

Now the whole life of a man is like the vapour of a caldron that makes itself visible for a little time and afterwards perishes. This is especially true in the case of the man who is a sinner. There is no profit whatsoever in the life of the man who works evil. If the rich man is a sinner, that fact shall be of no benefit to him. Have you never heard the words which Solomon spoke, saying, 'He who has come forth in vanity, shall also depart again in vanity; he who has come forth in grief, shall depart again in grief.' (Eccles. 6:4) Even as it is written, 'There shall be no joy to the wicked man, says the Lord.' (Isa 48:22) Again, 'The hope of the wicked man shall perish.' (Prov 11:7) Again, 'The wicked man shall be like the dust which the wind drives along before it on the face of the ground.'

Show me now, O sinner, what kind of pleasure is it that comes to you during your whole life? If you say, 'I have been a rich man all my life and I have passed my time as one,' then I shall say to you very gravely, 'What kind of pleasure was it that came to you during all the time in which you were living in sin?' If you are rich in gold and silver, what advantage is that to you, for you were produced from the earth? Truly, such a man eats and drinks today but tomorrow he is carried off in the midst of his riches.

Show me, O sinful man, what kind of rest it is which you find. You occupy yourself all your time in lending money at usury and in trafficking in merchandise. You build houses and stalls for sheep and cattle, you plant vineyards, you become a merchant, and sail the seas with your wares, and yet you are at all times like the man who is in agony of his death. You oppress the poor and deceive the stranger. You rob the houses of widows and amuse yourself by day and by night, and yet the bread that you eat is like that of every other man. While you are occupied in doing these things, the period of your life that is appointed to you comes to an end, and you are rejected, like a sour grape.

The possessions that you have heaped together shall remain on this earth and the sins that you have committed shall go before you to the throne of God. The images shall provide the proofs of your folly and the houses that you have built others shall dwell in. As for your soul, because of your lawless behavior, they shall carry it away into the outer darkness. From the vineyards that you have planted, others shall gather in the grapes. You yourself in Hades shall eagerly desire that the juice of it be dropped upon your tongue to cool it.

In your lifetime you amused yourself by day and by night and you were weary because of the multitude of your possessions. At your death you departed to the punishment that is never-ending, in exchange for your wickedness. Moreover, if the sinner is a poor man, you will find that he works both by day and by night because of the insistence of his poverty. You will find his son hungry and naked and his wife sick and afflicted with the suffering of infirmity. You will find them quarrelling and cursing each other and there is no peace at all between them. They are occupied by day and by night; they live in tribulation with their children. The man longs for death a thousand times over because of the suffering that is inside him. He sees the poverty and suffering of his wife and the misery of his children and he commits sin yet more and more. He commits thefts and swears false oaths, even as it is written, 'Poverty humbles a man.'

He adds sin to sin and he spends his life doing this until the appointed span of his life comes to an end. Then he is carried away suddenly, heavily laden with the load of his sins, and he comes forth into poverty. Show me now what kind of benefit it is to a man of this kind to be born into the world, for there is nothing in it but suffering and wretchedness and sorrow. It was concerning such a man that were written the words, 'He who has come in emptiness (or, vanity) shall depart in emptiness (or, vanity), and his name shall be proclaimed in the darkness,' (Eccles 6:4) whether he be rich or poor. Woe to those who are born into the world, for the deceitful deeds that they have done in the world shall be a punishment for them. What comfort (or, consolation) shall there be to the man who shall die in his sins? There is nothing for him except suffering and sorrow in this world and in the next. Have you not heard what is written in the Book of Isaiah the prophet, 'The sinner that shall live for one hundred years shall be accursed'? (Isa 65:20)

Tell me, O man of sin, when it was that you enjoyed yourself. Did you, perhaps, enjoy yourself in your mother's womb? If so, what kind of enjoyment did you have? You were shut up in the darkness and in the humour of her body, and you did not know when it was day, or when it was night. Did you, perhaps, enjoy yourself when you came forth from your mother's womb? If you did, what kind of enjoyment did you have? From the moment in which you were brought forth, you cried and wailed. Had you been comfortable you would not have wept for weeping belongs to suffering and pain. Did you, perhaps, enjoy yourself when you were being suckled at the breasts of your mother? If you did, what kind of enjoyment was it? You wept at all times, and you had no heart. Did you, perhaps, enjoy yourself when you were a small child? If you did, what kind of enjoyment was it? Your face was cast down at all times to the earth, you crawled about on your hands and feet, your mouth was always wet with the saliva which trickled from it, and when a beast might have attacked you and killed you, you were ignorant of it.

Did you, perhaps, rejoice when your legs gained firmness, and you could walk? If you did, what kind of enjoyment was it? Your parents taught you first, and then they sent you to the master craftsman that he might teach you a trade by which you might earn a living. Did you, perhaps, rejoice when you grew up and arrive at man's estate? If you did, what kind of enjoyment was it? The lust of early manhood that was in you was fighting against you, and never for one moment did it cease to goad you. Did you, perhaps, enjoy yourself when you took a wife? No, no, you could not enjoy yourself, for you burdened yourself with heavy cares. Did you, perhaps, enjoy yourself when you begot children? If you did, what kind of enjoyment was it? You loaded yourself with cares both by day and by night. For the man who has married a wife and has begotten children has never a moment's peace; on the contrary, his head is always burdened with cares, especially if he is a poor man, for then his tribulations are doubled.

Did you, perhaps, enjoy yourself when you became an old man? If you did, what kind of enjoyment was it? Your bones became broken, the light of your eyes was extinguished and your teeth became loose and incapable of chewing food. Your heart ceased to have perception and to understand a word of wisdom, your nerves, sinews, and tendons of the body failed, and ceased to work without difficulty. Your mouth lost its shape and was unable to utter words distinctly, your voice became feeble, and the ears lost their power to hear. All these things came upon you in your old age, but more especially there came great tribulation of heart, because you were drawing near to the grave, and you did not know how long men would enquire after you. Will you, perhaps, rejoice when the span of life that has been allotted to you has come to an end, when you must go before God? What kind of enjoyment will you have when that moment comes? You will cast yourself down upon your bed in your tribulation of heart, a great wave of heat will envelop you, and the attack of sickness will become more violent, and you will heave sighs over your sins, because you have no good deeds to your credit. You will weep for your little children who shall become orphans, and you will be greatly disturbed because of the calamity that has come upon you. You will look at the Powers with terrifying faces that have come after you, and you will sigh over the end of your life, because it has drawn near so speedily. Perhaps you will rejoice, O man, when you stand before the throne of God? What kind of enjoyment will you have there being laden with your load of sins and having not one good deed before you?

The avenging angels (or, executioners) shall seize your soul and shall gnash their teeth at you. Your sins shall follow you closely and shall be your accusers. Where will you turn your face, O wretched man? What manner of place will you look for in order to find rest in it? You shall find it neither on the right hand nor on the left. Behold the poor whom you have wronged! Behold those who were in misery, and the strangers whom you defrauded and ate up what goods they had! Behold the false oaths! Behold the slandering! Behold the hatred! Behold the envy! Behold the contentions! Behold the impurities! Behold the pollutions! Behold the fornications! Behold the murders and all the rest of the evil deeds that you have committed! At that moment, the Judge shall cry out, 'Cast him into the outer darkness, where there is weeping and gnashing of teeth.' (Matt 13:42; 25:30)

This is the end of all the men who are sinners and

who have not repented of their sins before their deaths. Behold, I have made the matter quite clear to you and have shown you that there is no profit in the life of man who is born into this world. If you wish for salvation, make haste and redeem your sins by means of acts of charity and by works of compassion to the poor. Even if you have committed every kind of sin, turn back and repent and God shall forgive you, for He is compassionate and He loves mankind.

He says, 'I do not desire the death of the sinner, but rather that he should turn back from his evil way, and repent and live.' (Ezek. 18:23; 33:11) Again He says, 'If the transgressor has turned back from his wickedness, and does righteousness, I will no longer remember the wickedness which he has committed, but he shall live through the righteousness which he has done.' (Ezek. 17:27) He says, 'Turn back to Me, O children who have gone afar off, and I will heal you of your wounds.' (Jer 3:22; 30:17) He says by His mouth that is full of life, 'I have not come to invite the righteous, but the sinners to repentance.' (Matt 9:13; Mark 2:17; Luke 5:32) Again, 'Come unto Me every one who is suffering, and is laden, and I will give rest to you.' (Matt 11:28)

Thus you may see, O man, the love for man that

God shows towards us. Finally, waste not day after day, month after month, and year after year, for the span of life that has been allotted to you is coming to an end, and you must depart, laden with the load of your sins. I have declared all these things out of love for you because of the verse which is written, 'Man is born to trouble.' (Job 5:7) Now it was because the prophet thought that there was no profit in a man's life, but only suffering and misery, that he said, 'Man is born to trouble, and his days pass quickly.'

Concerning the righteous, their whole life is joy and gladness, and since they have been born to blessedness, they shall also depart to the blessedness that is perfect. Truly, happy and blessed is the righteous man who is born into the world! Blessed is the man who is righteous and merciful, for he shall eat of the good things of the earth, and shall enjoy the kingdom that is in the heavens. Blessed is the poor man who gives thanks and who is meek and gentle, for he shall go forth from the poverty of this world, and shall receive riches that are never-ending. In very truth this is the man whose sorrows shall come to an end, and who shall inherit the rest that shall never end. It is written, 'Blessed are the poor in spirit, for to them belongs the kingdom which is in the heavens.' (Matt 5:3) Again, 'Blessed is the man whom You shall receive to

Yourself, O Lord.' (Ps 65:4) Again, 'Better is one day inside Your courts than one thousand passed outside them.' (Ps 84:10)

Behold now, we say these things to you, O my beloved, for the admonition of the soul. I know, however, that the tears which have come forth from your eyes shall become to you a fountain of salvation, which shall cleanse your bodies on the day of the great festival of Saint Victor the General. Believe me, O God-loving congregation, I have no wish to set in motion this word which is full of tribulation, and I would not introduce sadness into the festival of Saint Victor, had it not been that my mind was carried away by my thoughts, and it seemed to me as if I saw the General standing before me. He raised up gladness in my heart and mind, in his love towards us, and he spoke to me, saying, "O man, speak to this congregation for the salvation of their souls. You shall bring them into the haven of salvation on the day of my commemoration, and they shall repent of their sins. This result will afford me far greater happiness than ten thousand encomiums. I do not wish to receive the honour which belongs to this world, for my justification is in the heavens, before my Lord and my King, Christ."

When I had heard these words from Saint Victor, and

saw the care which he took for all those who are heavy laden, I at length turned my tongue towards you, O my sons and my daughters, and I spoke these few words to you for the welfare of your souls. Now, therefore, let us send before us the things which we find for the benefit of our souls in the day of need, so that Saint Victor, may make supplication on our behalf before Christ. It is written, 'His counsel is more to be chosen than gold, and the precious stone of very great price.' (Ps 19:10; Prov 8:10, 11, 19) According to Paul, 'Let us pay good heed to the things that we hear, lest we fall away.' (Heb 2:1)

If, O man, you have sinned through thoughtlessness, turn, repent and God shall forgive you. Again, if you have not committed sin, take good heed to yourself that the Devil be not envious of you, for he is a deceitful villain and he hates the race of man. You heard what is written in the Catholic Epistle, 'Be sober, watch; for your adversary the Devil goes roundabout roaring like a lion, seeking to swallow up your soul.' (1 Pet 5:8) Again, Paul says, 'Our strife is not against blood and flesh, but against principalities and powers, and against the governors of the world in darkness, and against spirit beings of evil beneath the heavens.' (Eph 6:12) Our Saviour commanded us, saying, 'If the master of the house knew at what hour the thief was coming he would keep watch, and would not permit him to break into his house; even so do you yourselves watch, for you know not in what hour the thief will come.' (Matt 24:42-43; Mark 13:35; Luke 21:36)

Now you know well, O my beloved, that it is right for a man to keep watch by day and by night, so that the Devil may not be envious of him and may not destroy his righteousness. Do not make a pretense and say, 'I have committed many sins and God will never forgive me, even if I do repent.' Take heed to yourself and do not talk in this way. Never let sin gain dominion over you. Even if you have committed a multitude of sins, turn, repent and God shall forgive you and He will number you with those who have never committed sin at all. You see how Saint Victor rejoices with us on this great festival, which we celebrate this day, and how he has prepared for us the table of the Spirit. Truly, this holy encomium is a healing medicine for us. The understanding of the Holy Scriptures is

a consolation to us. This encomium is a healer of every one for it strengthens those who stand and raises those who have fallen. As for us, let us keep carefully the things that we have heard and we shall find salvation.

Now I may narrate to you a few of the mighty deeds which have taken place in the martyrium of St Victor, which I have seen with my own eyes. Moreover, since certain of our inspired Fathers and Bishops who have lived before my time, that is to say, Eusebius, Julius and Innocent, undertook to declare your honour and the miracles which you performed in your martyrium, and were unable to proclaim your powers, how much less shall I, a humble man, be able to do so? How can I possibly pass over the sea of your splendid deeds? For this reason I lay my finger on my mouth: I do not know how to declare your gift of healing and especially because through your holy gift the disease which spreads over my legs and feet from time to time you have made to decrease in my body.

Great is the grace which God gives to you, and He has permitted these manifestations of healing to be permanent in your martyrium. That is to say, the dumb speak, the lame walk, the lepers are cleansed; you ease out devils and raise the dead through the mighty gift which God has permitted to be permanent in your martyrium. Hear now, and I will narrate to you the following great miracle to the glory of God and Saint Victor.

VICTOR AND THE VOW

There was a certain man in this city that owned very great possessions, large flocks and herds, sheep pastures and vineyards. This man was exceedingly good and kind to the poor and he had such a firm belief in Saint Victor that every year he used to give a large quantity of wine to the shrine of the saint. His offering remained always in the shrine of the holy man during the whole course of his life. The Good God, at the request of Saint Victor, blessed the man, and he became rich, and exceedingly prosperous. The blessing of God shone on his house and on his gardens, vineyards, meadows, fields and possessions. The man increased his alms and oblations which he used to give to God in the name of Saint Victor. His wealth still continued to increase greatly and his flocks and herds were exceedingly choice and fine. At length he fell ill of the sickness of which he died.

He called his son and said to him, "My son, behold I am going the way of all the earth. Be zealous in giving gifts to the poor and to every one who is in need, even as you have seen that I have been in the habit of doing. Take special care in respect of the offering to my Lord Saint Victor. You shall not diminish anything from it, no, you shall add to it; for it is he who has blessed us and has given to us these great riches. Let your charities and gifts be multiplied for they shall open to you the treasure houses of the kingdom which is in the heavens." His son answered and said, "Everything that you say I will do." Immediately the man sank back fainting and died.

His son took possession of his wealth but his heart was not perfect with God as was written concerning Solomon (1 Kings 11:1-10), and he was not charitable towards the poor. Finally he treated his father's will with contempt and he did not observe the commands that he had given to him. He diminished the charities and gifts that his father used to give, he ate and drank delicately and he put away from him the fear of God. When the season of the vintage arrived, the steward of Saint Victor sent certain clergy to him to receive the offering of first-fruits, according to the custom of his father. The son would not give them but said to himself, "It is not Saint Victor who drinks the wine, but it is the clergy who drink it; moreover, I shall certainly not give away this large quantity of wine, but I will put it aside and devote it to the needs of my own workmen." In this way he foolishly withdrew the offering from the saint and he did not remember that which is written, 'Charity seeks not its own.' (1 Cor 13:1) So he gathered in the grape harvest according to his father's custom and he discovered that the wine was so great in quantity that he could not measure it. He had it carried into storehouses, saying, "I will keep it until the time when the merchants of Palestine come to visit my father this year, and I will give it to them, and will take in exchange from them much goods." What did Saint Victor do to him that had neglected to give him his offering through love of possessions? Suddenly St Victor made the wine change and it bred worms became putrid and sour. All the man's affairs went backward, but he did not know that it was the hand of God that was upon him.

It came to pass that on a certain day the merchants arrived and they brought him a large quantity of gold with which they wished to buy some of his wine. When they had tasted the wine, they found that it was very bad indeed. Afterwards they opened other skins in the doorway of the wine storehouse and they found that the wine in them was worse than that which they had tasted before. In short, they tried all the wine and they found that it was quite worthless. They said to the young son, "Truly we marvel at this wine and wonder what has happened to it since your father has become blessed. Perhaps it is that you have neglected it. In any case, we do not know what has happened to it." After saying that, the merchants took the gold from him again and returned to their own country. The son was very sad indeed and grieved exceedingly. After some days, the son became conscious of the sin that he had committed and that it was Saint Victor who had destroyed his property because he had neglected to supply his holy offering. He was saying, "Woe is me, because I did not listen to the words of my father, and because I allowed greed to blind my eyes. I wished to bring the offering of the martyr into his hand and behold, he has destroyed all the possessions that were mine. What shall I do from this time onwards? I do not know."

During that night, Saint Victor came to the man in unspeakable glory and he said to him in a very threatening manner: "Since the love of money has shut your eyes and you have stolen the offering which your father used to give to God in my name, behold I, even I, destroyed all the produce of your vineyard. I made your wine to become full of worms and putrid. I will destroy your vineyard and it shall not yield for you its fruit because of your audacity. Assuredly because you neglected to give the offering to my shrine, I myself made all your wine perish."The man was greatly moved and he said, "My lord, who are you that you are surrounded by such exceedingly great glory?" St Victor answered and said, "I am Victor the General. I am he who blessed the possessions of your father. I multiplied for him his corn and wine. I doubled for him his flocks and herds, his possessions and his goods, because of the alms and oblations that he gave to the poor, and the offerings that he made to God in my name. You, however, inasmuch as you have not obeyed your father, and have not remembered the fear of God, but have been zealous in the stealing of the offering from my martyrium, I myself have punished you, and have destroyed your labours.

In you has been fulfilled that which is written, saying, 'A city is founded by the compassion of a mighty man, and it is uprooted through the folly of the fool.'" (Prov 11:10-11)

When the man had heard these words, he cast himself down upon his face, saying, "Forgive me, O my lord, you holy martyr. I have sinned beyond the measure of all mankind's capacity of sinning, but do not count up my sins. I will become your servant and will fear you, even as my father did, until the day of my death. I promise your holy splendour that, if you will show compassion to me and forgive me my impudent deeds, I will give one half of my substance and flocks and herds to your shrine this year. The other half I will give to the community and to the maintenance of those who work on my estate. Besides these I will add to the charitable gifts which my father used to make to the poor." The saint said to him, "God has removed your sin and this shall be to you a sign that He has done so. When you rise up tomorrow morning open the door of your wine cellars and taste your wine and you shall find that it has turned to a proper, settled condition. Thus shall you know that God is able to do everything and that it is the blessing of God that makes men rich.

God is not in need of your gifts and charities and of your offerings, but He does desire that you should display a right course of action in respect of Him. Have you never heard that which is written, 'He who shows mercy to the poor lends to the Lord,' (Prov 19:17) and 'Pay your vows to God, and let every one who is round about Him take a gift to Him'? (Ps 50:14; 76:11; Nah 1:15; Deut 23:21; Job 22:27) Now, therefore, take heed to yourself and do the things that have come forth from your mouth. I will make supplication to God on your behalf that He may make your riches to be as great as those of your father. When you shall go forth from the body, your soul shall not be set apart for punishment because I will carry it as a gracious thing into the presence of God. Have you never heard what is written,

'The supplication of the righteous man is exceedingly mighty and affects much'? (James 5:16) Now, therefore, O my son, watch yourself well from this day forward and farewell!"

When the saint had said these words to the man, he ceased to see him. Straightway he woke up in his dream and was very much moved and he told the things which he had seen to his people and they marveled. When the morning had come, he opened the door of his wine cellar and he found that his wine was exceedingly excellent. He proclaimed the mighty deeds of Saint Victor throughout the whole city. He summoned the steward of the saint to him and he gave to him half of his produce according to what he had vowed to the saint. From that day onward he became a very zealous man and he was exceedingly anxious about the salvation of his soul.

Thus you see, O my beloved, that the mighty deeds of Saint Victor, whose festival we are celebrating this day, are truly great, and that my feeble tongue is incapable of declaring one in ten thousand of his virtues and honours. Let us celebrate his festival this day in purity of heart and body. He is sufficiently strong to pray for us to the Lord, to forgive us our sins. Let us withdraw ourselves from every evil thing and from every kind of fornication. Let us not continue in our sins so that our visitation may not come to an end. Remember that the world shall pass away and the desirable things of it, but he who performs the will of God shall live forever. (1 John 2:17) Therefore let us not establish ourselves upon the hope which is vain, for the Apostle says, 'The hope which is seen is not hope.' (Rom 8:24) That is to say, the riches of this world shall pass away like the snow. Do not be a man of violence, for no violent man shall inherit the kingdom of God. Do not be a man of strife, for it is said that there is no profit in any man of strife.

Do not be a lover of money for the root of all evil is the love of money. Do not be a fornicator for him who shall defile the temple of God, him God will destroy. Do not be a liar, for God shall destroy every man who utters lies. Do not be a drunkard, for no drunkard shall inherit the kingdom of God. Do not be a man of lust, for it is said, 'Whosoever shall look at a woman to desire her has already committed adultery with her in his heart.' (Matt 5:28) Do not be an adulterer, for the adulterer destroys his soul. Do not be a lover of pleasure, for it is written, 'They loved pleasure more than they loved God.' (John 12:43) Do not be a babbling gossip, for a gag of fire shall be thrust into the mouth of the babbler. Do not be a hater of your brother, for he who hates his brother is a murderer. Do not be a man with a double tongue, for a double tongue is like a two- edged sword.

If you will observe these things in your own person, you shall be a servant of the Lord. Let us stretch out our hands to the poor in charity and compassion, for it is written, 'Blessed are the merciful, for they shall obtain mercy.' (Matt 5:7) Let us visit the sick and those who are shut up in confinement, in order that God in His compassion may visit us. Let us put clothing on the naked, in order that we may escape from the trouble and the gnashing of teeth. Let us receive into our houses the poor, who have no houses, on the festival of Saint Victor, so that he may remember us before God. Let us break every bond of violence, and every bond of enmity, and every bond of wickedness in respect of each other, in order that God and His holy angel will be at peace with us.

At this point, we must give pause to our discourse because the time is come when we must perform the service of the Holy Offering. It is true that our discourse has run to an inordinate length, but the people were thirsty for the waters of the word of God and for the narrative of the mighty deeds of the saint. It shall happen for us that Saint Victor shall make entreaty to God on our behalf that He may forgive us our sins, through Jesus Christ, our Lord, to Whom be glory, forever and ever Amen.

COLOPHON

This book was copied through the zeal and care of the most God-loving deacon Pourot. He undertook the preparation of it and presented it to the church of Saint Victor of Tebo, that is of Apollinopolis, according to the speech of the Alexandrians. May God preserve for life and health the God-loving brother Pourot and make him worthy of the joy of the kingdom which is in the heavens. May he live the angelic life that he has assumed, even as our fathers did, the ancestors of our community and may he pour out his blessing upon us and upon all the saints likewise! Amen.

May the Lord Jesus Christ, Who is in very truth our Real God, preserve for life and salvation the most God-fearing arch-presbyter Aba Abraham, the president and director of the Monastery of Saint Mercurius of Tebo and may he pour out his blessing upon us. May the Lord preserve for life and salvation all the fathers and sons of the monastery and make us worthy of their blessing. May He incline their hearts to pray for me before our King, Christ. May He forgive me my sins which are many and may He show mercy to me in the day of my visitation, to me Joseph, the least of all men and the most miserable, the son of the blessed Sisinnios, the Archdeacon of the Catholic Church of Saint John the Baptist in the city of Snê. May the Lord give peace to him, and to Zôkratôr, the least of all men, the deacon, the son of Joseph the deacon. Pray for me. Amen.

Written on the eighteenth day of the month Parmouti, in the six hundred and sixty-seventh year of Diocletian (A.D. 951).